Diversity

The Natalie Zemon Davis Memorial Lecture Series at Central European University, Vienna

Series Editor: Jan Hennings

Published in the series

- Lynn Hunt, *Measuring Time, Making History* (2007)
- Miri Rubin, *Emotion and Devotion: The Meaning of Mary in Medieval Religious Cultures* (2009)
- Eva Österberg, *Friendship and Love, Ethics and Politics: Studies in Mediaeval and Early Modern History* (2010)
- Ute Frevert, *Emotions in History: Lost and Found* (2011)
- William A. Christian Jr., *Divine Presence in Spain and Western Europe 1500–1960: Visions, Religious Images and Photographs* (2012)
- William C. Jordan, *Men at the Center: Redemptive Governance under Louis IX* (2012)
- Katherine Verdery, *Secrets and Truths: Ethnography in the Archive of Romania's Secret Police* (2013)
- Peter Burke, *Hybrid Renaissance: Culture, Language, Architecture* (2015)
- Averil Cameron, *Arguing it Out: Discussion in Twelfth-Century Byzantium* (2015)
- Joan Wallach Scott, *In the Name of History* (2019)
- James S. Amelang, *Writing Cities: Exploring Early Modern Urban Discourse* (2019)
- Leslie Peirce, *A Spectrum of Unfreedom: Captives and Slaves in the Ottoman Empire* (2021)
- Carlo Ginzburg, *Secularism and Its Ambiguities: Four Case Studies* (2023)
- Magda Teter, *Blood Libels, Hostile Archives: Reclaiming Interrupted Jewish Lives* (2025)
- Ulinka Rublack, *Dürer's Coats: Renaissance Men and Material Cultures of Social Recognition* (2025)

Diversity

The History of a Wandering Value

Lorraine Daston

CEU PRESS

Central European University Press

Budapest–Vienna–New York–Amsterdam

Cover illustration: Carla Peeters, *A Bouquet of Flowers* (ca. 1612). Oil on panel. The Metropolitan Museum of Art, New York. Public domain.

Cover design and lay-out: Sebastian Stachowski

ISBN 978 90 4857 479 7
E-ISBN 978 90 4857 545 9 (pdf)
E-ISBN 978 90 4857 546 6 (accessible ePub)
https://doi.org/10.5117/9789048574797

Table of Contents

List of Figures *vii*

Introduction
What Makes a Value Valuable? *1*

Chapter One
Diversity as an Aesthetic Value *7*

Chapter Two
Diversity as an Economic Value *47*

Chapter Three
Diversity as a Political Value *81*

Endnotes *115*

Bibliography *127*

Index *137*

List of Figures

Fig. 1.1: Pliny's exotic peoples. Source: Sebastian Münster, *Cosmographia universalis* (1544 or later editions). 22
Fig.1.2: Marco Polo and his brother meet Kubla Khan. Source: *Livre des merveilles* (ca. 1420), Bibliothèque nationale de France, MS Français 2810, ch. 6. 27
Fig. 1.3: Turkish Gentlewoman at Home. Source: Nicolas de Nicolay, *Discours et histoire veritable des navigations, peregrinations et voyages, faicts en la Turquie* (1586), p. 65. 29
Fig. 1.4: Imperial drummer in the retinue of Charles V (ca. 1531). Source: *Das Trachtenbuch des Christoph Weiditz*, Table X. 30
Fig. 1.5: Jewish doctor (Istanbul). Source: Nicolas de Nicolay, *Discours et histoire veritable des navigations, peregrinations et voyages, faicts en la Turquie* (1586), p. 115. 31
Fig. 1.6: *Wunderkammer*. Source: Frontispiece, Ferrante Imperato, *Dell'Historia naturale* (1599). 33
Fig. 1.7: Aztec nobleman at the court of Emperor Charles V (ca. 1531). Source: *Das Trachtenbuch des Christoph Weiditz*, Table XIX. 44
Fig. 1.8: Asia, America, and Africa offer up their plant treasures to Europe. Source: Frontispiece, Carolus Linnaeus, *Hortus Cliffortianus* (1737). 43

Fig. 2.1: Divergence of character. Source: Charles Darwin, *On the Origin of Species* (1859). 49

Fig. 2.2: Pin factory. Source: Jean d'Alembert and Denis Diderot, *Encyclopédie, ou Dictionnaire raisonné des sciences, des arts et des métiers. Recueil des planches*, vol. 4 (1765), plate 1. 54
Fig. 2.3: Professions of Paris. Source: Claude-Louis Desrais, *Petits métiers parisiens* (late eighteenth century). Musée Carnavalet, Paris. 56
Fig. 2.4: The human body as factory. Source: Fritz Kahn, "Der Mensch als Industriepalast," *Das Leben des Menschen* (1926). Wilhelm-Fabry-Museum. Photo: Peter Siepmann. 59
Fig. 2.5: Tree of Life. Source: Ernst Haeckel, *The Evolution of Man* (1879). 65
Fig. 2.6: G.B. Sowerby, Structure of *Orchis pyramidalis*. Source: Charles Darwin, *On the Various Contrivances by which British and Foreign Orchids Are Fertilised by Insects* (1862), Fig. III, p. 22. 69

Fig. 3.1: Masthead motto of Frederick Douglass, *The North Star* (1848). Source: US Library of Congress. 82
Fig. 3.2: Google N-Gram "Diversity" (1900–2020). 83
Fig. 3.3: Google N-Gram "Diversity/Equality" (1900–2020). 84
Fig. 3.4: Racial Makeup of the United States. Source: US Census 2020. 91
Fig. 3.5: South African Flag (adopted 1994). 98

Introduction

What Makes a Value Valuable?

Our current landscape of values is balkanized. Values that once traveled arm-in-arm—the elegant scientific theory that was also the true theory; the fairy-tale princess who was as good as she was beautiful; the business that reliably turned a profit because it treated its workers well—now need a passport to cross the borders between the various realms of value. And, as often as not, values that try to exit their assigned realms are likely to be turned away at the border by a gimlet-eyed philosopher eager to prove that their passports are forgeries. Since the late eighteenth century, the True, the Good, and the Beautiful rarely keep company, and inferences drawn from one realm of value to another are ipso facto suspect. Scientists may still hanker after simplicity and symmetry in their theories, but these aesthetic values no longer carry epistemic force. Businesses would no doubt prefer to do well by doing good, but economic values such as efficiency and productivity and ethical values such as humane working conditions and generous sick leave are usually framed as either-or trade-offs. Useful beliefs are too often in tension with true beliefs, as anyone who has tried to persuade someone else to give up a dearly held conviction by presenting the evidence against it can testify. Whoever proposes to admit values from one normative realm—aesthetic, economic, epistemic, ethical—into another is immediately suspected of conducting an illicit smuggling operation. Dual citizenship is not an option.

This at least is the official version of how values should work in the post-Kantian philosophical dispensation. The borders of the various normative realms are in principle sealed. We do not expect the rich to be good (rather the contrary) or the truth to be pleasing (all our facts seem to be disagreeable). Yet unofficially, as with all borders, there is a fair amount of traffic back and forth. Values do seem occasionally to wander from one realm to another. Frugality in the economic realm—getting the most out of the least—can turn into elegance in the aesthetic realm (the minimalism of a haiku) or parsimony in the epistemic realm (Occam's razor as applied to explanation). Very occasionally, these wandering values become more valuable as they migrate, bringing along the capital accumulated in other realms with them. Although officially forbidden, dual or even triple citizenship in multiple normative realms confers advantages, just as it does for the fortunate holders of multiple passports.

This book is about the career of one such wandering value, diversity. Originally an aesthetic value in ancient, medieval, and early modern times, it also became an economic value in the late eighteenth century and later also a scientific one in the context of biodiversity in the mid-nineteenth century and thereafter. From the mid-twentieth century onwards, it has assumed the additional status of a moral and political value, closely associated with justice in many institutions and polities. The argument can be simply summarized: instead of disqualifying diversity as a value, migration from one normative realm to another has only made it more valuable.

The argument is pursued episodically in the book's three chapters, each chapter devoted to diversity's career in a distinct normative realm. Chapter 1 describes how diversity first emerges in antiquity as an aesthetic value, a form of beauty first associated with the extravagant proliferation of forms and colors of flowers but soon generalized from natural history to human workmanship and indeed to human beings themselves. Far from being a marginal aesthetic value, the useless beauty of diversity became the core of modern aesthetic philosophy in Kant and later among the Romantics, epitomized in the motto, "art for art's sake." Chapter 2 shows how diversity, originally associated with wastrel excess, became an economic value of frugality and efficiency through its association with the division of labor in Enlightenment political economy. But instead of shedding its original associations with nature's cornucopia of forms, diversity as an economic value became the core of Charles Darwin's evolutionary explanation of speciation. Chapter 3 charts the startlingly swift rise of diversity as a moral and political value in the late twentieth and early twenty-first centuries, especially but not exclusively in the context of court cases relating to university admissions. Debates over diversity as a form of justice are still raging as I write, and it is beyond the competence of the historian to predict, much less to adjudicate their outcome. But historical analysis can illuminate why diversity as a political value spread so quickly and so widely, in contrast to the older but still struggling value of equality. Unlike equality, diversity as a political value could piggy-back on its established status as an aesthetic and economic value.

The wandering value of diversity stands as a provocative counterexample to reigning accounts of distinct normative realms with sealed borders. Not only has diversity repeatedly breached these borders; its normative authority as a value also appears to have been boosted by its wanderings. I am aware that it is a single case, and therefore potentially an anomaly and certainly no basis for sweeping generalizations about the nature of values per se. But anomalies can be good to think with, because they reveal the limits of and preconditions for the general rule. One such anomaly can sharpen the eye for others, and I hope that this brief book might catch the eye of other historians interested in how values wax and wane but also wander. Perhaps the book may also be of use to the philosophers, sociologists, and anthropologists who have thought deeply about the sources of normativity—what makes a value valuable—in providing an example of the fungibility of value across normative realms. Most of all, I hope that readers of this book will find it clarifying in thinking through their own values and why they hold them.

The chapters in this book were originally delivered as the Natalie Zemon Davis Lectures at the Central European University in March 2025 and are presented here in the form that I delivered them. Each of the chapters might easily be expanded into three or four more; the examples I have given are meant to illustrate the over-arching argument rather than to present a complete history of the value of diversity over two millennia. The lecture format has the advantages of distillation and clarification: theses must be stated more crisply; examples must be chosen more carefully. This starker presentation makes the argument stand out, and if I have the opportunity to return to this topic, I hope to benefit from the criticisms that such an exposed position is likely to elicit.

My final words must be ones of thanks. I am grateful to the Central European University for its gracious hospitality, and especially to Professor Jan Hennings, who has shepherded these lectures from initial invitation to publication with great tact and good humor. I also thank Sina Buchholz and Josephine Fenger for their invaluable help in preparing the manuscript of my lectures for publication.

It would have been an honor under any circumstances to deliver lectures named for Natalie Zemon Davis, one of the greatest historians of our age. It was also a personal pleasure for me to be granted an opportunity to commemorate in some meager fashion the inspiration Natalie's brilliant work has provided for my own and still more the extraordinary kindness with which she welcomed me and a handful of other young women faculty members to Princeton University in the mid-1980s. Had she lived to attend and comment upon these lectures, as was her wont, I am sure she would have turned them upside down, inside out, and returned them to me utterly transformed and immensely improved. I miss her, and my name is legion.

Chapter One

Diversity as an Aesthetic Value

Introduction: The Diversity of Diversity

You find yourself amidst a gathering of people: in a classroom, at a meeting, in a museum, at a sporting event, or just on the corner of a busy street, waiting with the other pedestrians for the light to change. Look around you: are the people gathered wherever you happen to be a diverse group? And diverse in what way—by age, by gender, by ethnicity, by hairstyle, by dress? Or by characteristics not so easily observed at a glance —by politics, religion, profession, mother tongue, social class, or taste in music? And why pose the question in the first place: why do we care about diversity, however we define it? In other words, why is diversity a value? These lectures are an attempt to answer that last question from a historian's perspective.

Some of you may well be wondering, isn't it self-evident that diversity is a value, and isn't any effort to historicize such a value—to show that it did not always enjoy that self-evident status—ipso facto an effort to undermine it? It is entirely understandable, especially in the current fractious political context, that my project should arouse such suspicions. Diversity, both the value and the programs justified in its name, is indeed under attack in many quarters, and not just from the parties of the reactionary right. The liberal left entertains its own worries about the effects of diversity initiatives on its traditional values of universalism and human rights. Moreover, ever since Nietzsche, any project purporting to provide morals with a genealogy has been accused of subverting all morals. The testimony of history, as well as that of travelers and ethnographers since Herodotus, reveals how varied the values of human cultures in different times and places have been. In a famous passage, Herodotus describes how the Persian king Darius summoned Greeks and Indians to his court and first asked the Greeks whether anything could persuade them to eat the bodies of their dead parents, and then asked the Indians what price they would charge to burn the bodies of their dead parents. Both sides recoiled in utter horror from the customs of the others, and Herodotus concludes that everywhere in the world "custom is the king of all."[1] Although Herodotus pointedly did *not* use this story to argue for cultural relativism and the arbitrariness of all customs, others have done so ever since. If values differ so flagrantly from one culture to another, and from one epoch to another, what value can be vaunted as valid everywhere and always? History has proved almost as corrosive to the claims of absolute, eternal values as anthropology. In the past fifty years, starting with the publication of Michel Foucault's *La volonté de savoir* (1976), history has indeed been used to challenge the self-evidence of ideas and values long believed to be dictated by nature and therefore immutable, especially in the realms of sexuality and gender roles. It is therefore not fanciful to imagine that any proposed history of the value of diversity, much less any attempt to question its self-evidence, is in fact a veiled challenge to that value.

Let me reassure you. I come neither to praise nor to blame the value of diversity but rather to explain it. What I will seek to explain is both the remarkable speed with which diversity established itself as a value in the moral and political realms since the 1990s and also why diversity has proved so difficult to define, despite its apparently now settled status as a self-evident moral intuition. Contrast this almost overnight success with the fate of equality, a much older value dating back to at least the eighteenth century in European political theory and even farther back in other traditions, but a value that has demonstrably failed to put down deep roots in our moral intuitions—witness the half-heartedness of almost all efforts to eradicate social and economic inequality, even in socialist polities constitutionally committed to that goal. From the standpoint of the glacial pace at which new values usually appear and disappear, diversity has burst onto the scene with the suddenness and luminosity of a supernova. It has traced at warp speed the trajectory from an everyday synonym for any kind of variety, as applicable to brands of breakfast cereal as to shapes of seashells, to essential term in our moral vocabulary. In universities, businesses, and governments, diversity has become an avowed goal. And not only avowed, but, in most cases, sincerely embraced: diversity has become a genuine moral intuition, viscerally felt, not just intellectually acknowledged. In stark contrast to the values of racial and gender equality, much less economic equality, which have taken centuries even to be recognized as values and which have yet to attain intuitive self-evidence or even legal guarantees, diversity conquered almost as soon as it arrived. Why and how that could happen is the subject of this book.

My argument is that the value of diversity has a much longer history than we realize. Whereas it is now a moral and political value, understood as closely akin to justice, it was previously first an aesthetic value and later an economic one. Part of the self-evidence that the moral value of diversity enjoys builds upon those earlier foundations, now sunk below the level of collective consciousness, like the remains of an ancient city buried beneath its modern counterpart. Just as an archaeological excavation can expose the remains of ancient Rome or Varanasi to view, a closer look at the both the imagery and the arguments that ground today's value of diversity can disclose traces of those earlier chapters in the history of the value of diversity. And just as these modern cities are both literally and figuratively supported by their ancient architecture and lineage, so our current value of diversity in the political realm is supported by its past career as first an aesthetic and then an economic value, the topics of chapters 1 and 2, respectively. Chapter 3 examines the recent transformation of diversity into a political value, roughly between 1980 and now. Its conclusions must remain tentative, because these developments are still unfolding as this book goes to press. My aim is not to take up arms on either side of the current raging debate over diversity. I am a historian, neither a commentator on the present nor a prophet of the future. But my hope is that a deep history of the value of diversity in the past can illuminate the present and perhaps even offer guidance for the future.

One further ambition of this brief history of diversity as a wandering value is to query the hard-and-fast boundaries currently drawn between different realms of value—aesthetic values, utilitarian values, epistemic values, and moral values. Whether with regrets or with relief, philosophers since Kant have largely abandoned the classical equation of the good, the true, and the beautiful, and Kant's three critiques—on epistemology, ethics, and aesthetics—stand as monuments to the division of this once united realm of values into three separate kingdoms. Although there have been occasional efforts to form alliances between these three kingdoms—for example, when scientists prefer simplicity and symmetry in their theories or politicians argue that efficient measures also best promote human welfare—no one now argues for a necessary connection between the true and the beautiful in science or the good and the profitable in politics. In fact, to claim value in one realm—for example, the aesthetic—is often seen as ruling out claims to value in another realm—for example, the moral.[2] We resist any easy inference from a beautiful face to a good soul, or from a useful belief to a true one. If anything, we may well bet that the probabilities are in favor of a negative correlation among such values.

But the case of diversity as a value that has historically wandered among these realms should make us rethink their strict separation, or so I shall argue. Not only is diversity simultaneously an aesthetic, moral, economic, and arguably also an epistemic value; its recent meteoric rise as a moral and political value depends in part on its past and present history as a value in other realms. Being acknowledged as a value in any realm may turn out to bolster that value's status in other realms. If the case of diversity is anything to go by, value may be less like the marble in which values are often allegorized in sculptures and more like water, able to flow almost anywhere and to assume the shape of almost any vessel into which it is poured.

Whether this general and abstract argument about the nature of value itself holds water can only be illustrated, not proven by the specific case of the wandering value of diversity. This book is first and foremost a history and therefore about concrete particulars. In this chapter, I follow the trail of diversity as an aesthetic value, from ancient meditations on the extravagant proliferation of flowers and gemstones to medieval curiosity about the diversity of human beings to Renaissance collections of the wonders of art and nature as an expression of wealth and power.

Nature at Play: Flowers and Gemstones

It is in the nature of encyclopedias to pile up diverse particulars on all and sundry topics, and the most famous encyclopedia of Greco-Roman antiquity, Pliny the Elder's *Natural History* (ca. 79 CE), does not disappoint. For over 1600 years, readers reveled in the "20,000 noteworthy facts" about nature that Pliny had collected in thirty-seven volumes about everything from the 91 kinds of vines and grapes (book XIV) to the docility of elephants (book VIII) to the history of gold coinage (book XXXIII) to the medicinal properties of various waters to increase fertility or mend broken hearts (book XXXI)—and much, much else.[3] Pliny's nature is a cornucopia of abundance and variety. But nowhere in this vast and varied compendium does Pliny marvel more at nature's fecundity than in the chapters of the *Natural History* that treat the diversity of the forms and colors of flowers and gemstones, nature's gorgeous ornaments. Like all ornaments, flowers flaunt their impracticality. Their proliferation of delicate shapes and vivid colors is an over-the-top extravagance. Workaday nature produced all other things "because of their usefulness," according to Pliny, but when it comes to flowers, nature goes on holiday: "here she is in her most sportive mood, playful in her great joy at her varied fertility."[4]

In contrast to the durability of most of nature's productions, flowers wither in a day, which Pliny, who had a strong moralizing streak, took as "an obvious warning to men that the bloom that pleases the eye most is the soonest to fade." Elsewhere in the *Natural History*,

Pliny devoted whole volumes to the uses of plants—as food, as drugs, as dyes, and as textiles. One of Pliny's declared aims was not simply to catalogue nature's productions but to describe how they can serve human purposes. Even gemstones, another occasion for Pliny to rhapsodize over how "Nature's grandeur … evokes more wonder in the minds of many men who set such store by the variety, the colours, the texture and the elegance of gems," do not entirely violate the otherwise universal principle of utility. Pliny disdained amber as the only exception to the rule that every substance "lends itself either to display or to practical use," but even the despised amber allegedly cured ear infections.[5] In contrast, flowers are nature's baubles, as fragile as they are beautiful and as pointless as they are various. The very diversity that dazzles the eye divorces the multifarious forms from function.

Flowers were for Pliny and his successors the premiere example of pure aesthetic value, unadulterated by any use except to adorn in gardens and garlands. More durable gemstones could at least be used as repositories of exchange value (Pliny cited the eye-watering prices of some particularly large jewels, such as a beryl ring worth two million sesterces),[6] easy to store, transport, and, if need be, hide. Other ancient, medieval, and early modern lapidaries extolled the virtues of various precious and semi-precious stones: amethysts promote sobriety and sound intellects; coral healed epilepsy; pearls fortified weak hearts; onyx caused excess saliva and nightmares.[7] In the late seventeenth century, the English natural philosopher and chemist Robert Boyle, albeit cautious, still thought it plausible that certain gems might have healing properties, citing the case of a gentleman acquaintance cured of chronic nosebleeds by a bloodstone.[8] No such claims could be made for flowers, which were too ephemeral to be hoarded and traded and whose fragrant and healing essences could be extracted only by crushing the beautiful blossoms (for example, the flowers of foxglove, *Digitalis purpurea*, used to treat heart disease). Flowers seemed to exist in all their motley diversity solely to delight the eye.

Flowers were nature's art—indeed, flowers were nature's gauntlet thrown down to art. Marveling at the diversity of flowers, Pliny declared that "[n]ot even the painter's art, however, suffices to copy their colours and the variety of their combinations."[9] Aristotle had claimed, "Nature does nothing in vain," and most naturalists ever since have heartily agreed. But like the peacock's tail that famously sickened Charles Darwin because of its apparently useless beauty, a dangerous extravagance in the struggle for existence, flowers seemed to defy utility.[10] More than just a challenge to artists to beat nature at its own game, flowers display an exuberance of form and color that seems to ratify an aesthetic of art for art's sake. Almost two thousand years after Pliny, when Immanuel Kant in 1790 cast about for an example of beauty that commands admiration just because it serves no purpose and can be subsumed under no concept, what first came to mind were not paintings and sculptures but flowers.[11] Flowers were more than nature's own artworks; they also evoked the purest, freest aesthetic judgment. No wonder artists were envious.

Flowers therefore became an arena for the rivalry between art and nature, daring artists to new heights of mimetic virtuosity. A long tradition stretching from antiquity through the seventeenth century portrayed nature as a superior artisan whose workmanship and powers of invention outstripped all human skill and inspiration.[12] Artists who vied with nature were therefore at a disadvantage. Yet already in ancient Greece stories circulated about great artists who proved their mettle by their astonishingly accurate renderings of flowers. The ancient Greek artist Pausias (fourth century BCE) allegedly fell in love with Glycera, a maker of flower garlands, and in painting the portrait of his beloved became a legendary portraitist of flowers.[13] To imitate flowers as faithfully as possible in art could in some cases be an act of religious devotion. Some of the earliest *trompe l'oeil* techniques in late medieval illuminated manuscripts featured flowers that bloomed at pilgrimage shrines, blossoms hallowed by their proximity to a saintly relic or sacred site.[14] For centuries, from Pausias' portrait to Albrecht Dürer's *Blau blühende Schwertlilie* (1503), the depiction of flowers occasioned some of the most advanced mimetic techniques in art.

The mimetic aesthetic centered on the diverse beauty of flowers reached its zenith in the Dutch still life paintings of the seventeenth century, in part because Dutch gardeners were the most successful at cultivating new species of flowers imported from early modern European commercial and imperial excursions to Asia, Africa, and the Americas.[15] Tulips, originally from the Levant, were only the most famous of the exotic flowers for which the Dutch created both a market and an art form, the still life of a bouquet of flowers overflowing its vase (itself often an expensive import of Chinese porcelain) and surrounded by other exotic luxuries, such as half-peeled oranges, baroquely shaped seashells, and Persian carpets. Nor were the skillful Dutch horticulturalists content simply to naturalize imported flowers such as tulips from Turkey and calla lilies from South Africa in a cooler climate; they became expert at breeding dozens of new varieties that diversified the prodigious diversity of flowers still further. Some of the tulip cultivars that fetched the most astronomical prices at the height of the Dutch tulip craze, like the red-flamed Semper Augustus, also commanded center stage in the still life bouquets.[16] Confronted with such blooming confusion in the garden of the Dutch banker George Clifford, the Swedish naturalist Linnaeus thundered against the florists who had deceived botanists into enumerating "93 [species of] Tulips (where there is only one) and 63 Hyacinths (where there are but two)."[17]

But what was a nightmare to the taxonomist was a boon to the artist. Just because flowers represented nature's showiest display of the aesthetic of diversity, the most perfect imitation of flowers became the highest aim of artists bent on beating nature at its own game. Flower still life paintings did nature one better. Not only did the virtuosi of this genre capture the subtlest tints and most delicate textures of nature; they concocted bouquets that combined flowers that would never bloom simultaneously in nature: spring tulips with summer roses; blossoms from northern gardens with tropical fruits like pineapples and oranges.[18] Both impossible and immortal, these ever-fresh painted bouquets outdid nature, whose flowers were doomed to wilt and die. Cornelis de Bie, seventeenth-century connoisseur of Dutch painting, wrote in praise of the Utrecht flower painter Jan Davidsz de Heem: "De Heem paints, Nature is amazed."[19]

Nowadays neither mimesis nor the genre of the floral still life enjoys anything approaching its seventeenth-century prestige in the arts. Since the invention of photography, mimesis has been demoted from supreme proof of artistic virtuosity to a merely mechanical process. Modern artists of note still painted flowers, as in the case of Piet Mondrian's striking *Red Amaryllis with Blue Background* (ca. 1907), but their fame seldom rests upon those works. Yet the same Romantic era critics who condemned mimetic genres like landscape painting and still life as plodding efforts to reproduce nature exactly, unembellished by the artist's imagination—these same critics nonetheless clung to the aesthetic of art for art's sake, in the service of neither truth nor morality nor utility.[20] Nor did the close associations of that aesthetic with diversity disappear in the modern era, despite the rejection of mimesis and the demotion of flowers. Rather, the diversity of form and color that had made flowers emblematic of this ancient aesthetic broadened its scope to embrace what we would now call cultural and biodiversity. Biodiversity is the subject of chapter 2, but because human diversity would eventually become so central to contemporary understandings of diversity as a moral value, the history of how earlier epochs assessed and appreciated the differences among peoples and cultures is essential to understanding the ramifications of diversity as an aesthetic value.

Ancient, medieval, and early modern Europeans would have encountered other peoples and cultures primarily in word and image, but also occasionally in person, on pilgrimages to holy shrines, through trade and commerce with distant lands, on military campaigns, and in the parades of enemy captives and booty after victorious wars. Travelogues like those of Herodotus (ca. 484–ca. 425 BCE) about Egypt and Babylon and of Marco Polo (ca. 1254–ca. 1324) about the Mongol empire and Yuan dynasty China, encyclopedias like Pliny's *Natural History* and Isidore of Seville's *Etymologiae* (ca. 625 CE), and accounts of the military conquests of emperors from Alexander the Great (356–323 BCE) and Julius Caesar (100–44 BCE) to the Habsburg Charles V (1500–1558) fed a voracious public appetite for details about strange people in strange lands. None of these accounts was stranger or more influential than that of Pliny, whose descriptions of the customs and physical appearance of the peoples of the Roman empire and beyond were endlessly recycled in travelogues, sermons, histories, and entertainment literature until the end of the seventeenth century.

The visible signs of human variation are probably objects of universal human curiosity, but which visi-

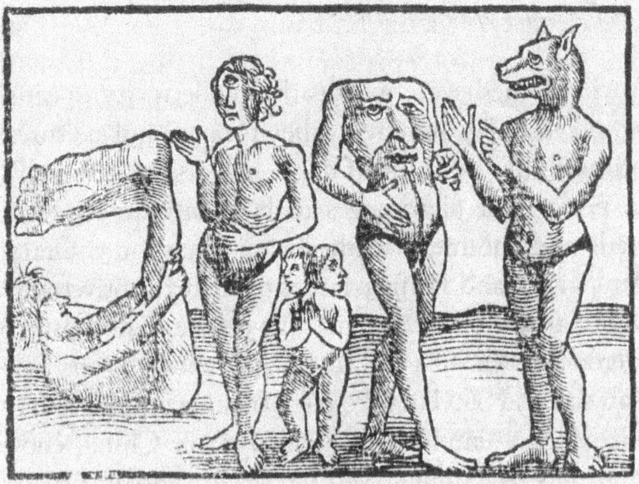

Fig. 1.1: Pliny's exotic peoples. Source: Sebastian Münster, *Cosmographia universalis* (1544 or later editions).

ble signs matter to whom and why is almost as variable as human beings themselves. Whereas modern attention to diversity focuses on race, ethnicity, religion, and sexual orientation, Pliny barely mentions such features. And no wonder: his attention is riveted by the much more spectacular differences in human appearances reported in his sources about the peoples[21] who allegedly inhabited the rims of the Roman world, in Scythia, India, Libya, Ethiopia, and the northern lands beyond the Alps (Fig. 1.1). There were the Indians who were over twelve feet tall and never spat or suffered from headaches or toothaches; the Arimaspi of the far north beyond the Alps who had only one eye in the middle of their foreheads; the tribe of dog-headed humans in the Nulus mountains (possibly the Himalayas); the umbrella-foot people, who had only one gigantic foot, which they used as a parasol to shield themselves from the sun; the headless Blemmyes of Nubia whose faces were on their chests—not to mention the Androgynes of Libya, whose left breast was that of a man and whose right breast that of a woman and who reproduced hermaphroditically.[22] This last example is about as close as Pliny gets to a discussion of sexual diversity, although he was very interested in cases of reproductive diversity—cases of triplets and even quintuplets, the oldest man and woman to beget children, traits that are and are not inherited.

He was even less interested in skin color. The subject was briefly mentioned in his *Natural History* not in the context of human variety but rather in an account of latitude, lengths of night and day, and climate. One consequence of exposure to more or less sunshine, Pliny wrote, was complexion: near the equator, Ethiopians were scorched by the sun, with curly hair, and were made wise by their climate, while the inhabitants of the far north were made pale as frost, blond, and fierce by theirs. In the temperate latitudes, a Goldilocks mean between the two extremes produces people "of medium bodily stature, with a marked blending even in the matter of complexion; customs are gentle, senses clear, intellect fertile, and able to grasp the whole of nature."[23] Not coincidentally, Pliny's own Roman stock happened to inhabit these fortunate middle regions between icy pole and fiery equator. Pliny's preference for the intermediate shade of light-brown or olive skin and abhorrence of extremes (whether too dark or too light) seems to have been widely shared in the ancient Greco-Roman world.[24]

Neither in the account of different skin colors or of the more outlandish peoples who live on the margins of the ancient Roman world did Pliny anywhere suggest that these people were less than fully human, however odd their outward appearance. Although the Blemmyes, Cyclops, Androgynes, and other bizarre peoples would be later lumped together as the "monstrous races," Pliny did not describe them as monsters, reserving that term for individuals whose malformations were interpreted as portents specific to the particular time and place at which they were born—an interpretation that could not be plausibly applied to whole peoples. The full humanity of the Plinian peoples was cemented into Christian doctrine by Saint Augustine, one of the many later authors who plundered Pliny's *Natural History* for marvels, and who made a point of asserting that the Blemmyes and company all had rational souls and could therefore be candidates for conversion and salvation. All were descended from Adam, the first human being, and therefore each was a "rational and mortal being ... however extraordinary such a creature may appear to our senses in bodily shape, in colour, or motion, or utterance, or in any natural endowment, or part, or quality." Just as Pliny concluded his chapter on these peoples with praise for nature's marvels, Augustine concluded his retailing of the same material with praise for the beauty of God's design, as a whole and in its "constituent parts, in their likeness and diversity."[25] When the probably fictitious English knight Sir John Mandeville claimed to have run across Pliny's dog-head people (Cynocephales) in the Nicobar Islands in Southeast Asia, he reported that "[t]hese people, despite their shape, are fully reasonable and intelligent."[26]

Pliny's views on the link between climate and both skin color and temperament enjoyed a long afterlife.[27] Well into the eighteenth and even nineteenth century, climate, interpreted as proximity to the equator or poles, was invoked to explain both bodily and cultural differences among peoples.[28] However, Pliny's very brief remarks on the subject were supplemented by a far more extensive medical literature on color and complexion derived from Greek and Arabic sources and widely taught to medical students throughout Latin Europe by the twelfth century. These texts dealt with the color of skin, eyes, and hair as observable indices of the balance of humors in an individual, not of a whole people. The original meaning of complexion referred to the proportions of the four humors—red blood, white phlegm, black and yellow bile—that defined the bodily type and psychological temperament of a person.[29] One widely taught elementary medical text, the *Isagogue* (composed as an Arabic commentary on Galen in ninth-century Baghdad and translated into Latin in the late eleventh century) distinguished among five skin colors, including red, white, yellow, black, and gray, but added further nuances, depending on external temperature (hot or cold) and emotional state (anger, fear). Although an individual's basic complexion (for example, sanguine if blood predominated among the humors, or melancholy if black bile did) was relatively stable, it could be altered by all manner of factors, from illness to a bad scare. But as historians of medicine have pointed out, the most important context for noting variations of color for premodern physicians was not skin color but urine, of which up to 42 shades might be distinguished by the discerning clinical eye.[30]

Medieval and early modern European ideals of the most beautiful human coloring divided more along gender than along racial lines. Women were ideally blonde, dark-eyed, and endowed with a snow white/rose red complexion. But for men, a pale complexion was a badge of shame, an indication that they shied away from the hardy, outdoors life of the soldier and the hunter.[31] Even scenes of Adam and Eve in Eden, before the invention of sun screen or even clothes, observed the convention of pale female and tanned male. Black was occasionally associated with the demonic by some early Christian writers, such as Origen (ca. 185–ca. 253 CE), but there were also black Christian saints, such as Saint Maurice and one of the three kings of the nativity, Balthasar, who by the fifteenth century was consistently represented by artists as black. The premodern world abounded with ethnic stereotypes and prejudices,

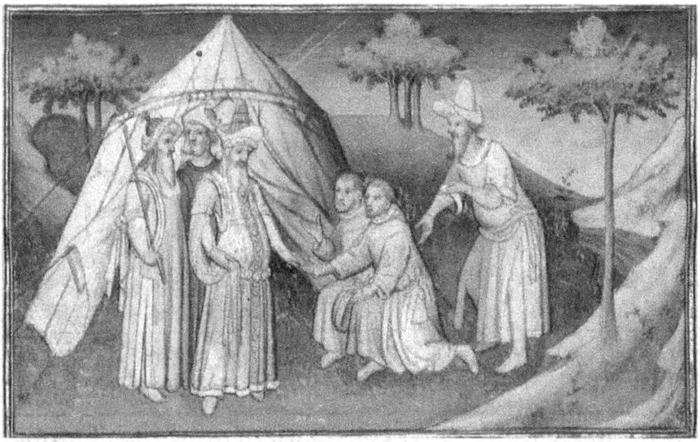

Fig.1.2: Marco Polo and his brother meet Kubla Khan. Source : *Livre des merveilles* (c.1420), Bibliothèque nationale de France, MS Français 2810, ch. 6.

but these were rarely imagined in terms of bodily features like skin color. In medieval visual depictions of foreign peoples, the key visible markers of ethnic identity were clothing and hairstyle: turbans and beards for Muslim Saracens and other Asians; short hair, no beard, and bare heads for Latin Europeans (Fig. 1.2).[32]

The keen interest in the variety of what might be called the second skin of ethnic dress, as opposed to the first skin those clothes covered, only intensified in the sixteenth and seventeenth centuries, when European commercial, imperial, and missionary ventures reached from Peru to Japan, from Lapland to California. A new genre, the profusely illustrated costume book, was among the most successful publications to issue forth from dominant printing centers (and commercial hubs) such as Venice and Nuremberg. Such books were soon translated into several European languages.[33] Images of Europeans and Ottomans, Asians and Americans featured in these books, which were often produced by travelers to these regions, such as the Augsburg artist Christoph Weiditz (ca. 1500–1559), who traveled to Spain and the Netherlands in the retinue of the Holy Roman Emperor Charles V, or Nicolas de Nicolay (1517–1583), gentleman of the chamber and royal geographer to King Henri II of France, who toured the Ottoman Empire as part of the French diplomatic delegation to the court of Suleiman the Mag-

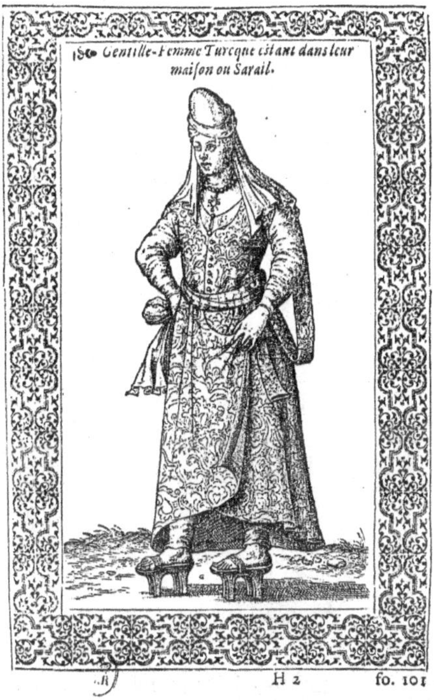

Fig. 1.3: Turkish Gentlewoman at Home. Source: Nicolas de Nicolay, *Discours et histoire veritable* (1586), p. 65.

nificent in Istanbul.[34] (Fig. 1.3) Curiosity about how other peoples in other places looked seems to have been richly reciprocated. For example, Japanese artists portrayed Portuguese merchants and Jesuit missionaries on fans and folding screens with the same fastidious attention to foreign dress and coiffure as European witnesses of the first Japanese visitors to Italy, who recorded in their accounts of the young Samurais their "white tunics embroidered with foliage and birds in gold … large and short silk trousers, very fine white socks … and very black hair" worn in a ponytail.[35]

As this 1585 description by an eye-witness to the arrival of the Japanese visitors in Bologna suggests, physical traits were noticed and remarked upon: just as the

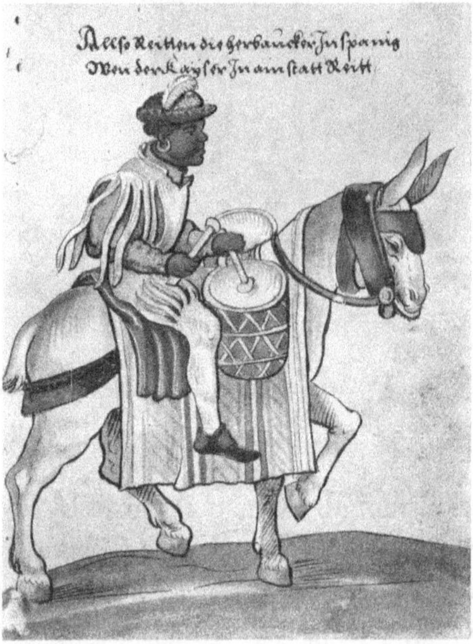

Fig. 1.4: Imperial drummer in the retinue of Charles V (c.1531). Source: *Das Trachtenbuch des Christoph Weiditz*, Table X.

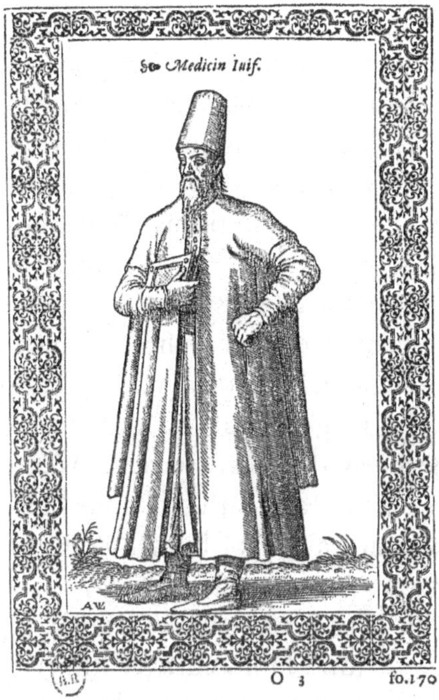

Fig. 1.5: Jewish doctor (Istanbul). Source : Nicolas de Nicolay, *Discours et histoire veritable* (1586), p. 115.

Italians were struck by the black ponytails of the Japanese, the Japanese underscored the big noses of the Portuguese. Weiditz painted the black skin of an apparently African drummer in the emperor's entourage. But it was his stylishly fringed doublet, slashed pantaloons, and feathered cap that probably riveted the gaze of observers (Fig. 1.4). However much they might have differed in language, customs, religion, and political system, the cultures depicted in the early modern costume books ordered relationships between men and women, master and servant, aristocrat and peasant, soldier and civilian, countryman and stranger by visible distinctions of dress (Fig. 1.5). These distinctions were usually enforced by sumptuary laws, which dictated who could wear what and on which occasions, often in minute detail. Social rank, profession, place of origin, and religion could be read off at a glance by those who knew the local conventions of costume.[36] For stay-at-home readers, the costume books paraded the astonishing variety of human cultures as a wondrous entertainment, much as Pliny's *Natural History*, Marco Polo's *Livre des merveilles* (1298), and *Mandeville's Travels* (mid-fourteenth century) had diverted earlier generations with marvelous tales of far-off realms. But for merchants, ambassadors, missionaries, and other go-betweens, whose success and even survival might depend on being able to decipher nuances of social standing in a foreign land without the help of a native guide or interpreter, the costume books were an invaluable vade mecum. Viewed in this light, it is not surprising that distinctions of dress by gender, class, religion, and profession, so fascinatingly diverse even within the same country, much less on different continents, eclipsed the comparatively minor variations in skin coloring or other physical features.

The Wonders of the World All in One Room

This image of a cabinet of curiosities—or what in German-speaking lands was called a *Wunderkammer*—crystallizes an irony of history. At precisely the moment when Pliny's evergreen popularity had begun to wither, as voyagers and naturalists debunked one after another of his marvelous tales of exotic peoples and

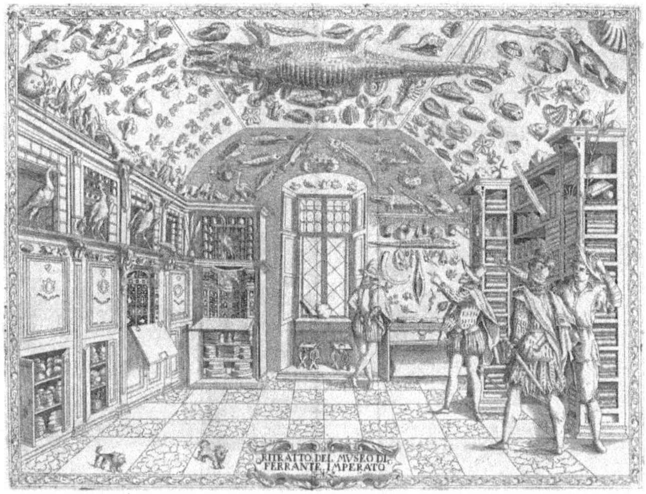

Fig. 1.6: *Wunderkammer*. Source: Frontispiece, Ferrante Imperato, *Dell'Historia naturale* (1599).

places as mere fantasies, Pliny's vision of the world as overflowing with the wonders of art and nature materialized in collections like this one all over Europe (Fig. 1.6). The reason for both sides of the apparent contradiction in Pliny's early modern fortunes was the same: the expanding reach of European commercial and imperial ventures to Africa, Asia, and the Americas undermined the credibility of many of Pliny's claims about far-off places at the same time that these expeditions brought back things just as wondrous as anything described in his *Natural History*—natural specimens such as armadillos, birds of paradise, and ruffled seashells; manmade articles such as intricate Mexican feather work, Chinese paper money, and Indian carved ivory. Novelties too delicate to be preserved, such as new varieties of tulips or shimmering butterflies from South America, might be represented in the collection by *trompe-l'oeil* paintings of exotic insects, flowers, and animals by the likes of the Flemish artists Joris Hoefnagel (1542–1601)—the paintings themselves small masterpieces of *trompe l'oeil* illusionism and therefore collectibles in their own right.

During the sixteenth and seventeenth centuries, the vogue for such collections cut across social ranks and institutions. Apothecaries like the Neapolitan Ferrante Imperato (1525–1615),[37] naturalists like the Danish professor of medicine Olaus Worm (1588–1654),[38] and scientific academies like the Royal Society of London (founded 1660)[39] gathered and exhibited specimens primarily of naturalia; libraries like that of Sainte Geneviève in Paris complemented their shelves of books with drawers stuffed full of coral, fossils, Chinese porcelain vases, and antiquities.[40] These collections advertised their holdings with published illustrations and descriptions that attracted visitors, and some, such as the collection associated with the anatomy theater of the University of Leiden, even printed multilingual tourist guides.[41] But the most spectacular of these collections were the ones least likely to publicize their holdings in word or image and the least open to casual visitors. These were the princely collections of the Electors of Saxony in Dresden, the archduke Ferdinand II of Tyrol at Schloss Ambras in Innsbruck, and the Habsburg emperor Rudolf II in Prague, to which were admitted only visitors of the highest rank, such as foreign princes or their plenipotentiaries. (The French essayist Michel de Montaigne [1533–1592] records with some pique in his travel diary the social slight of being denied a visit to the Ambras collection in Innsbruck, although he was a counselor of the Parlement of Bordeaux and a decorated courtier of King Charles IX of France.)[42]

The aim of such exclusive showings was to overwhelm the visitor with the floor-to-ceiling display of paintings by masters such as Dürer and Raphael, stuffed crocodiles and birds of paradise, coconut and nautilus shells worked in gold, stones that resembled plants, like coral, or animals, like fossils, monsters like two-headed snakes and oddities like a stag's antlers imbedded in a tree trunk, Japanese kimonos and Turkish clogs, and virtuoso workmanship of all kinds, from elaborate pocket watches to nested spheres of ivory. Because some of these items once housed in royal collections have survived to be exhibited at public museums like the Kunsthistorisches Museum in Vienna, we can still admire them as strange or beautiful or strangely beautiful individual objects. But we cannot experience the open-mouthed astonishment that a large room crammed with all of these objects arrayed in a vast miscellany must have evoked in the few privileged visitors allowed entry. Paintings of such collections, mostly imagined, can convey only the palest impression of these three-dimensional, total-surround spectacles of the fecundity of nature and art. Early modern princes knew how to alchemize such dumbstruck wonder into power and influence. As the young Francis Bacon (1561–1626) wrote in a student skit composed in 1596, a royal collection that included "a spacious and wonderful garden" stocked with all known wild and cultivated plants, salt and freshwater ponds for "like variety of fishes," a stable of "all rare beasts," and "a goodly huge cabinet" stocked with all the rarities wrought by art and nature would make the prince himself "the only wonder and miracle of the world."[43]

The *Wunderkammern* mark the zenith of the aesthetic of diversity. Eighteenth-century tastes rejected the extravagance and hodge-podgery of the *Wunderkammern* in favor of the restrained symmetries of neoclassicism; enlightened philosophers like Voltaire and David Hume disdained marvels as vulgar entertainment; naturalists like Linnaeus made mighty efforts to order the dazzling diversity of flora and fauna.[44] The national museums that inherited princely collections had already begun to segregate works of art from those of nature in the early nineteenth century, an arrangement epitomized by the two great buildings housing the Kunsthistorisches and Naturhistorisches museums in Vienna, both dedicated by Emperor Franz Joseph I in 1891. There has in recent years been a revival of interest in the *Wunderkammer*,[45] with some attempts to recreate those that have left a visible trace as well as a re-evaluation of such collections as repositories of biodiversity *avant la lettre*.[46] Although the rekindled fascination with the *Wunderkammer* aesthetic at precisely the moment when diversity of all kinds was vaunted as value is probably no coincidence, I know of no serious proposal to reunite the holdings of art museums and natural history museums. The modern appreciation of the cornucopia-like diversity on display in the *Wunderkammer* is always selective: biodiversity is no longer mingled with cultural diversity; ingenious works of art and nature are no longer displayed side-by-side; and the most curious of the curiosities have either been left to rot in storage or exiled to provincial museums. For example, the armor of Ferdinand II of Tyrol is on display at the Kunsthistorisches Museum in the capital Vienna, but the curious will have to go to Schloss Ambras in Innsbruck to see the antlers of a stag embedded in a tree trunk, although both items were once part of the same Habsburg collection that dazzled select visitors to the imperial court. Like the awestruck early modern visitors to the princely collections of the Habsburgs, we contemporary museum-goers shield our eyes from diversity at full-strength.

Conclusion: Empire and Diversity

Perhaps there is a deeper reason why we avert our eyes from diversity displayed at *Wunderkammer* intensity, a reason that goes beyond tidier tastes, beyond even discomfort at seeing a stuffed Laplander exhibited next to a narwhal horn. If there is a scarlet thread that weaves through the entire history of diversity as an aesthetic value, from Pliny's encyclopedia to Rudolf II's *Kunst- und Wunderkammer*, it is empire. Not only did Pliny dedicate the *Natural History* to the Roman emperor Titus; much of the material concerning, for example, the mining techniques of Spain or the architecture of northern Africa, came from his terms as governor of those provinces of the Roman empire, which at its greatest extent stretched from Britannia in the west to Babylon in the east and included all of what is now England, Wales, France, Spain, Portugal, Italy, Switzerland, Greece, the Balkans, Austria, Egypt, Turkey, Syria, and part of Germany, the north coast of Africa and the Arabian peninsula. The triumphal processions with which the Romans celebrated their conquests over other peoples were occasions for the display of war booty but also of human diversity in the form of enemy captives taken as slaves and animal diversity in the form of exotic animals.[47] Well into the eighteenth century, Prussian kings echoed this ancient imperial custom with parades of people of diverse ethnic origin or at least dressed up as such, as a symbol of world dominion long after the substance of the Roman empire had disappeared.[48] When Nicolas de Nicolay, the French ambassador to the Ottoman empire, praised foreign travel in the preface to his account of his voyage, his foremost examples were all emperors who had conquered the lands they visited: Alexander the Great, Julius Caesar, and Charlemagne. Christoph Weiditz's image of an Aztec arrayed in a feather cloak brought back to the court of

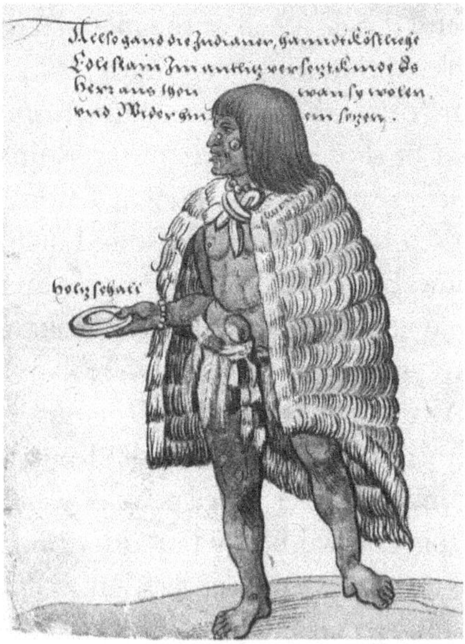

Fig. 1.7: Aztec nobleman at the court of Emperor Charles V (c.1531). Source: *Das Trachtenbuch des Christoph Weiditz*, Table XIX.

the Habsburg Emperor Charles V by the conquistador Hernán Cortes testifies to the imperial reach of the Habsburgs (Fig. 1.7). At its greatest extent, the Habsburg empire under Charles V included large parts of Central America, what is now Mexico, and the western parts of South America, as well as the Low Countries, Germany, Bohemia, Austria, Hungary, parts of France, the duchy of Milan and the southern half of Italy, Spain, Portugal, Sardinia, and Sicily, and the imperial collections drew upon all of these possessions. Paintings like Frans Francken the Younger's *Allegory of the Abdication of Charles V* (ca. 1635, now at the Rijksmuseum, Amsterdam) celebrated his global ambitions, symbolized by the allegorized continents kneeling at his feet and offering gifts of gold and gems, coral, an armadillo, porcelain vases, richly embroidered textiles—exactly the sort of gifts that might well end up in a princely *Wunderkammer*.

Distance had always been a proxy for the hallmarks of diversity, namely the exotic, the new, the rare, and the unusual. The appreciation of diversity among things commonplace and familiar was an acquired taste, and one that required an effort of intellect and will to sustain. When Pliny and after him Saint Augustine pointed out that no two human faces were identical, it was only to lament in the next breath that almost no one registered this familiar observation as the marvel of diversity that it was.[49] However diverse in fact, domestic peoples and products were seldom perceived as such. Familiarity bred, if not contempt, then oblivion. It took the shock of imports from elsewhere to dramatize the diversity of the world celebrated by Pliny's encyclopedia and early modern *Wunderkammern*. Commerce could and did supply such foreign imports by the boatload, but the safety of the ships that sailed from Lisbon to

Goa or Seville to Lima or Amsterdam to Java depended on the long arm of imperial protection to battle pirates, quash competition, and coerce foreign lands into trading relationships. Empire and emporium went hand-in-hand, then as now. Dominion over vast territories abroad also went hand-in-hand with increased diversity of things and people brought home. The correlation between empire and the aesthetic of diversity is not accidental.

And what about flowers, Pliny's first and favorite example of nature's ludic excess of forms and colors? A meadow of domestic wild flowers might have sufficed to illustrate nature's bounty, though we know that imported Egyptian and Persian cultivars also bloomed in Roman gardens. But from the botanical surveys of New Spain in the sixteenth century to the glasshouses of Kew Gardens (founded 1840) in the nineteenth century, great empires have always enriched gardens (and the florists who cultivated them) with flowering plants from elsewhere—tulips from Asia Minor, sunflowers from North America, rhododendrons from the Himalayas. Bioprospecting, as it is now called, has been historically driven by a demand for plants that can be used as drugs, such as the *Artemesia annua* of China, used to treat malaria, or the *Cinchona officinalis* of Ecuador, used to relieve fever.[50] As the Dutch tulip craze of the seventeenth century demonstrates, however, beauty

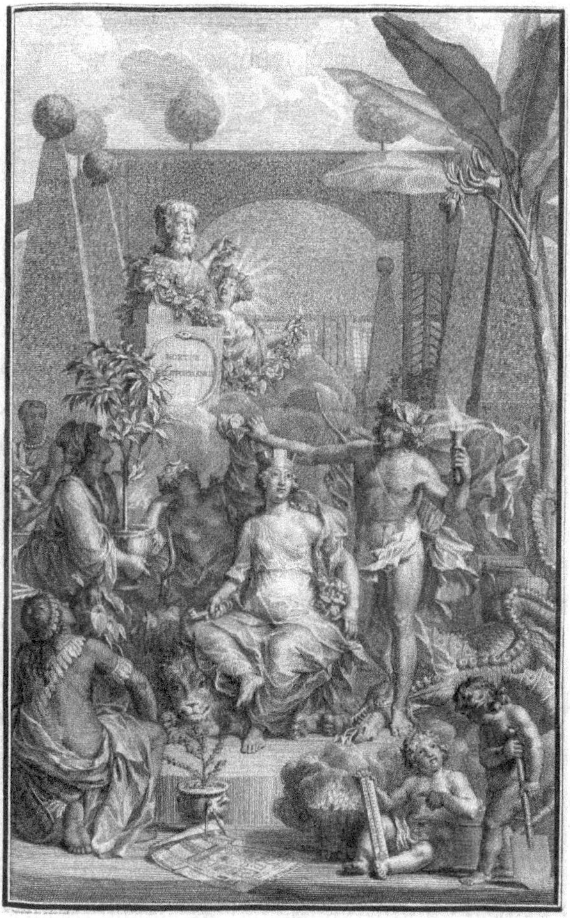

Fig. 1.8: Asia, America, and Africa offer up their plant treasures to Europe. Source: Frontispiece, Carolus Linnaeus, *Hortus Cliffortianus* (1737).

can generate its own lucrative market. The iconography of Linnaeus's first important publication, his catalogue of the extensive garden of George Clifford (1685–1760), a director of the Dutch East India Company, eerily echoes the motifs of those imperial allegories of the reign of Charles V (Fig. 1.8). The frontispiece of the *Hortus Cliffortianus* (1737) shows the enthroned allegorical figure of Europe, attended by the torch-bearing god Apollo trampling the dragon of ignorance underfoot, and surrounded by allegorical figures representing the Asia, Africa, and America offering up their choicest plants for Clifford's garden: "the most noble plants, fruits, flowers / That ASIA, AFRICA, and AMERICA can boast," according to the verses accompanying the image. To Apollo's left looms a banana tree, one of the hundreds of tropical plants that came Clifford's way via the Dutch East India Company, and the subject of an independent monograph by Linnaeus.[51]

These imperial associations should not discredit the aesthetic value of diversity, which has its own rationale in its vision of a cornucopia world, extravagantly ornamented with every form and color imaginable. But like every aesthetic value, that of diversity has historically had its peaks and troughs, and we should be alert to the preconditions for its moments of maximum intensity. At very least, global connections, whether commercial or imperial, manifested in the actual or imagined movement and mingling of peoples, favor the flowering of the aesthetic of diversity. I choose the word "flowering" here advisedly: whether blooming in a garden, painted in a still life, or mimicked in the coral and dendritic agate beloved of *Wunderkammer* collectors, the eye-catching diversity of flowers has been the prototype of this aesthetic value since antiquity. Chapter 2 describes how floral diversity broadened into all of biodiversity, but in so doing, transformed the value of diversity from an exaltation of the beauty of useless excess to praise for the utility of economic efficiency.

Chapter Two

Diversity as an Economic Value

Introduction: Endless Forms Most Beautiful and Wonderful

I begin with an ending, with the last sentence of the most famous book in the history of biology:

> There is grandeur in this view of life, with its several powers, having been originally breathed into a few forms or into one; and that, whilst this planet has gone cycling on according to the fixed law of gravity, from so simple a beginning endless forms most beautiful and most wonderful have been, and are being, evolved.[1]

The concluding words of Charles Darwin's (1809–1882) magnum opus, *On the Origin of Species* (1859), return us to Pliny's raptures over the endless forms most beautiful and most wonderful of flowers, gemstones, and indeed individual human faces. A sense of wonder at nature's seemingly inexhaustible creativity has been a leitmotif of natural history for millennia; natural history museums nowadays are at once a tribute to and a repository of what we now call biodiversity. Awestruck admiration of endless forms most beautiful and most wonderful is the unbroken line of descent that connects Pliny to Darwin and to all naturalists, from whatever culture and whatever century.

Aristotle, another great naturalist, once wrote that all philosophy begins in wonder, and by philosophy, he meant questions about the causes of things that evoke wonder, like the stars in the heavens and their regular movements.[2] Wonder at the diversity of natural forms did provoke both Pliny and Darwin into asking questions, but very different questions. As we saw in chapter 1, Pliny asked about the proliferation of the shapes and colors of flowers, so beautiful and yet so pointless. He concluded that nature delighted in diversity for its own sake, as a holiday from its more useful creations (and by useful, Pliny meant useful for human purposes). This vision of ludic beauty inspired the doctrine of art for art's sake, and for almost two thousand years, flowers remained the emblem of artistic freedom, the mind and hand at play. But Darwin asked a very different question. Look again at that final sentence of *On the Origin of Species*: "breathed into a few forms or one." Setting aside for the moment that timorous "breathed," a last sop thrown to the theologians, note the novelty

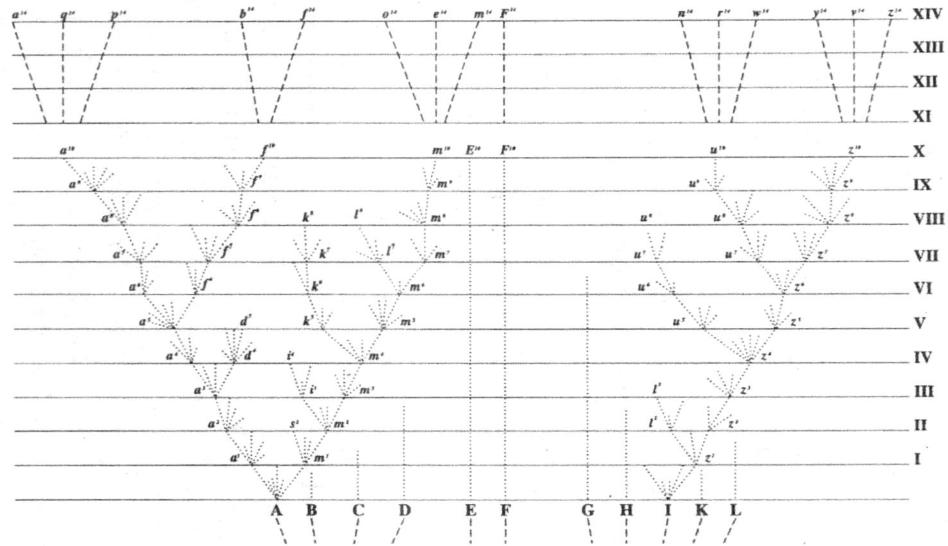

Fig. 2.1: Divergence of character. Source: Charles Darwin, *On the Origin of Species* (1859).

of what Darwin has set out to explain: not just the diversity of nature's forms but how diversity could result from a few or just one Ur-form.

Biologists since Darwin have understandably focused on the mechanisms of evolution, natural selection acting on heritable variability to produce new varieties and species. Conceivably, these mechanisms could produce a steady-state organic nature, in which some species go extinct and others take their place, as cosmologists once imagined a steady state universe, in which individual atoms pop in and out of existence, but overall, everything stays pretty much the same forever. Darwin's "few forms or one" conjures up an entirely different scenario, which is represented by the one illustration in his entire book: an all-purpose diagram that shows ever increasing diversification as a branching tree—or rather trees, each a different phylogenetic lineage (Fig. 2.1). Each twig sprouts yet more twigs (what is now called evolutionary radiation); where budding stops, so does the species (or genus or family or other higher-level taxon). Only one lineage (F) traces a straight line from beginning to end (let us imagine it as the lineage of the family *Limulidae*, the horseshoe crab, four species of which have survived since the Triassic, about 250 million years ago). Continuity of form over eons is the exception to the rule; the general motto of evolution appears to be "diversify or die." We can now rephrase Darwin's question, which asks: not only *how* does one form spawn many (the mechanisms of evolution), but *why*? Why "many"? Why diversify?

Taking Darwin's novel question as my departure point, in this chapter I trace how in the context of first economic theory and later evolutionary theory, the value of diversity itself mutated. From a long-lived aesthetic value epitomized by the wastrel profusions of flowers and the eye-popping miscellany of the *Wunderkammern*, diversity in the nineteenth century evolved into an economic value, epitomized by the division of labor on the factory floor. In contrast to its earlier associations with extravagance and excess, diversity came to be seen as way of maximizing efficiency. Finally, Pliny's question had an answer: diversity, even the diversity of flowers, was useful after all, albeit not to human beings, as Pliny would have required. Darwin wrote enthusiastically about how even the notoriously baroque forms of orchids could be explained by the selective advantages of cross-fertilization by the insects those multifarious shapes favored. But that still left Darwin with a question that has haunted evolutionary biology ever since: could the beauty of those endless forms be reduced to utility?

The development of Darwin's own thinking about biodiversity serves as a scarlet thread through the labyrinth of eighteenth- and nineteenth-century ideas about how human and natural economies create superabundance through the most ruthless efficiency. Darwin's intellectual journey was of course unique, and its final destination, the theory of organic evolution through natural selection, marked an epoch in the history of science. But many of the resources he drew upon were the common stock of physiology, natural history, and political economy of the late Enlightenment.

My story begins with the division of labor, a practice that dates back to ancient times but became central to conceptions of the advancement of civilizations and the increase in economic productivity during the Enlightenment. Analogies to the division of physiological labor among the specialized organs of animal bodies provided Darwin with the link to organisms with specialized adaptations to what he called "stations" (or ecological niches, in modern terminology). Such analogies could have been reconciled with older visions of nature's economy in the work of Darwin's anti-evolutionary predecessors, Carolus Linnaeus (1707–1778) or even Charles Lyell (1797–1875). But in Darwin's version, nature's economy was as savagely competitive as trade was at the height of the British empire, and as prone to drive some species to extinction as global trade was to drive some commercial firms into bankruptcy. Darwin's views on extinction cast a pall over earlier, rosier views of nature's fertility and diversity.

Both diversification and extinction in Darwin's theory were driven by the relentless pressure of natural selection, which weeded out all but the most useful adaptations. Darwin relished reducing the most spectacular examples of extravagant diversity of forms, namely orchids, to a shining example of exquisite adaptation in his monograph on the subject. Yet the problem of apparently useless beauty remained: what to do with the gorgeous but apparently worse-than-useless peacock's tail? In later works, Darwin added sexual to natural selection to deal with such cases, but his solution continues to leave many evolutionary biologists dissatisfied. In the conclusion to this chapter, I shall return to the enduring sense of wonder inspired by biodiversity among all who contemplate it, from Pliny to Darwin to biologists today: what to do with our lingering admiration for nature's workmanship, when nature is no longer Pliny's artist but just a collection of fixed laws, as blind as the law of gravity to the beauty of endless forms?

Nature's Factory

This pin factory in Normandy is one of the most famous scenes in the history of economics (Fig. 2.2). The image illustrates the article on "Épingle" in Denis Diderot's (1713–1784) great *Encyclopédie, ou Diction-*

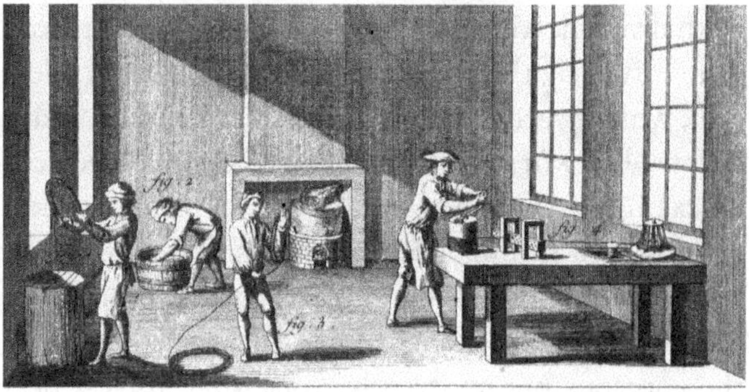

Fig. 2.2: Pin factory. Source: Jean d'Alembert and Denis Diderot, *Encyclopédie, ou Dictionnaire raisonné des sciences, des arts et des métiers. Recueil des planches*, vol. 4 (1765), plate 1.

naire raisonné des sciences, des arts et des métiers (1751–1765), the signature work of the Enlightenment. The article opens with an evocation of the universe in a grain of sand—or at least of complexity in a simple pin: "The pin is of all mechanical works the tiniest, the most common, the least valuable, and yet one of those that requires perhaps the most combinations ... for a pin undergoes eighteen operations before it enters commerce."[3] From the arrival of coils of metal from Hamburg or Sweden to the sticking of the finished pins, a dozen at a time, into paper slips, the article lays out the manufacture of pins circa 1750 step by step. Staffed by experienced workers, the factory could be mind-spinningly efficient, producing up to 48,000 pins per day. Influenced by this article, Adam Smith (1723–1790) began *The Wealth of Nations* (1776) with the pin factory as a shining example of how the division of labor promoted efficiency and technological innovation.[4]

The division of labor went on to have a meteoric nineteenth-century career, well beyond economic theory and industrial applications. It was a key inspiration for Charles Babbage's design of the first computer, as well as for Émile Durkheim's theory of the organic solidarity of advanced societies. The principle could be as readily applied to the factory assembly line as to the steps in a computer program—or to the differentiation of functions in a bustling city, in which cobblers make shoes, tailors make clothes, masons lay bricks, apothecaries make drugs, bakers bake bread, and so on (Fig. 2.3). By the mid-nineteenth century, the division of labor became a keystone of political economy and almost synonymous with efficiency.

But for our purposes, the most consequential application of the principle of the division of labor was to the life sciences, first to physiology and then to evolutionary theory. Specialization by task or function might produce diversity—all those different jobs that kept Paris running—but it did not produce beauty. It was the biologists who discovered how to connect the old

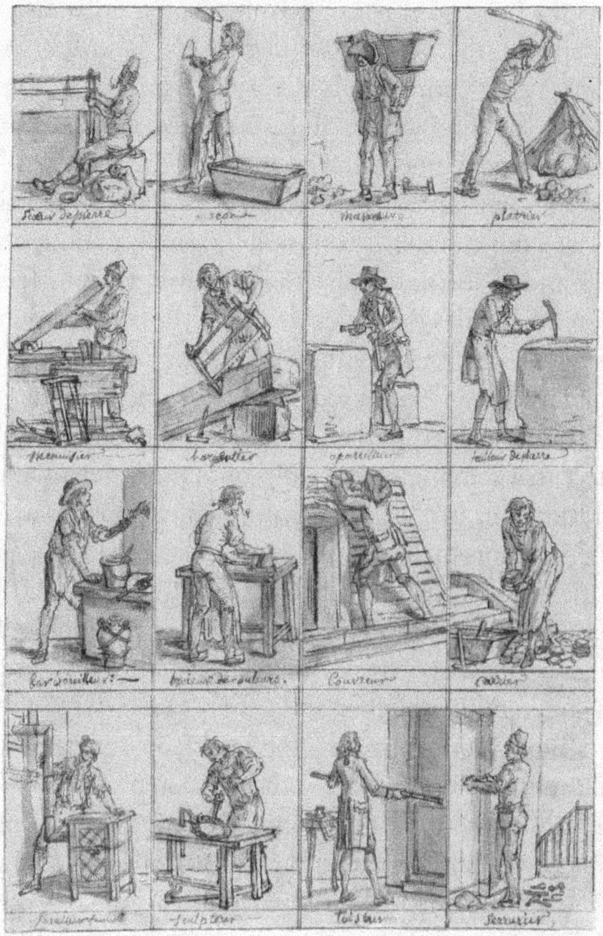

Fig. 2.3: Professions of Paris. Source: Claude-Louis Desrais, *Petits métiers parisiens* (late 18th century). Musée Carnavalet, Paris.

diversity of beauty in nature with the new diversity of efficiency in human society—and indeed to use the one to explain the other.

The French physiologist and comparative zoologist Henri Milne-Edwards (1800–1885) was the beneficiary of the vast natural history collections amassed during the eighteenth and early nineteenth centuries, as well as of the efforts made to bring some classificatory order into what had seemed to be the infinite variety of living organisms. The first edition of Linnaeus's wishfully named *Systema naturae* (1735)—no one at the that time could be sure that there *was* a system of nature—ran to only 12 pages; by the time the multi-volume twelfth edition (1766–1768) appeared, all the new species discovered in the meantime had swelled the total to 2,300 pages. As new observations and specimens arrived from correspondents and travelers all over the world, Linnaeus scrambled to keep his classification scheme from buckling under the weight of what we would call biodiversity and Linnaeus called "the Almighty's masterpiece."[5] Milne-Edwards was similarly overwhelmed by the "diversity ... which seems to be the primary condition imposed on nature in the formation of animals." But beneath the prodigal variety of nature's forms, Milne-Edwards detected a fundamental organizational principle, the division of labor:

> One sees that in the creations of nature, as in the industry of man, it is above all by the *division of labor* that perfection is obtained.

The body of humans and other complex organisms was, Milne-Edwards claimed, exactly analogous to a modern factory: every organ was specialized to a specific function, just like the workers in the pin factory. Stomachs did not think, and brains did not digest (Fig. 2.4). Milne-Edwards drew the paradoxical conclusion that it was precisely nature's "tendency toward economy" that produced the dazzling diversity of forms. The 7,000 then-known species of birds seemed to exhibit the most extravagant diversity of form and color; yet nature had achieved this result at "little cost," by working and reworking "the same materials" to different, ever more specialized ends.[6]

In *On the Origin of Species* (1859), Darwin made Milne-Edward's insight his own and used it as the foundation of his theory of speciation, once again invoking the division of labor:

> The advantage of the diversification in the inhabitants of the same region is, in fact, the same as that of the physiological division of labour in the organs of the same individual body—a subject so well elucidated by Milne Edwards … So in the general economy of any

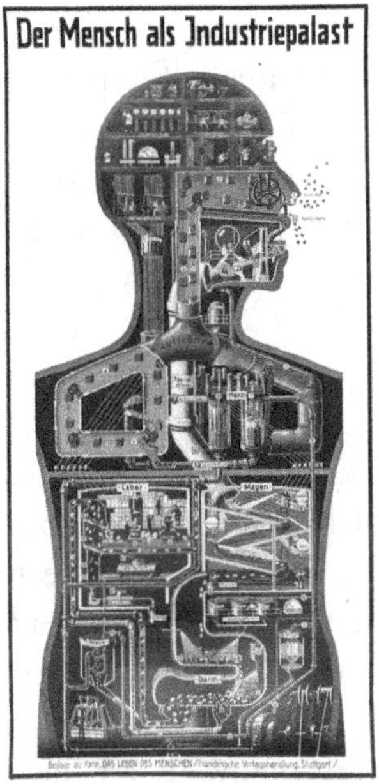

Fig. 2.4: The human body as factory. Source: Fritz Kahn, "Der Mensch als Industriepalast." Wilhelm-Fabry-Museum. Photo: Peter Siepmann.

> land, the more widely and perfectly animals and plants are diversified for different habits of life, so will a greater number of individuals be capable of there supporting themselves.[7]

Nature was no longer a *Wunderkammer* but an economy run on the most efficient principles to yield maximum productivity; no longer a playground for nature's fertile fancy but an arena of ferocious competition for scarce resources. Yet in Darwin's account of speciation, diversity-as beauty and diversity-as-efficiency merged: Pliny's wondrous cornucopia of natural forms merged with Adam Smith's pin factory.

Efficiency and Extinction

Long before Darwin, economic metaphors had permeated natural history. But the meaning of economy also mutated in the early nineteenth century. The great Swedish naturalist Linnaeus had imagined all of nature as what he called an *oeconomia*. Although this word shares a Greek root, *oikos* (household), with the more familiar "economy," it was in many ways even closer to another derivative from that same root, "ecology," defined as a community or system of different species that co-exist in a relationship of well-ordered interdependence or equilibrium. Or as Linnaeus defined *oeconomia* in 1749, it is "the all-wise disposition in relation to natural things, by which they are fitted to produce general ends, and reciprocal uses."[8] In 1760 Linnaeus elaborated these ideas of balance and reciprocity in his closely related conception of *politia naturae*, or "police of nature," appealing to the eighteenth-century sense of "police" as measures taken by municipal authorities to insure prosperity and order. But this time, he focused on the forces that threaten to capsize nature's tidy household. The "police of nature" were "[t]hose laws of nature by which the number of species in the natural kingdoms is preserved undestroyed, and their relative proportions kept in proper bounds." Linnaeus worried about sharp-elbowed species, the kind that proliferated so vigorously that they threatened to crowd out their neighbors. If congregated all in one place, plants would soon overwhelm all other creatures. Fortunately, divine providence had assigned different kinds of plants to different "stations," as Linnaeus called them, analogous to the different stations of society, each occupying a different habitat and fulfilling a different task that contributed to the harmony of the whole. Linnaeus pursued this conceit of stations in nature and stations in society to almost comical lengths. The grasses are the sturdy "yeomanry" of the plant world, "trodden underfoot and oppressed," but thriving in adversity; trees are the "nobility," which tower above their "fellow-citizens" and shelter them from the elements; herbs are the landed gentry, "the luxuriance of their foliage, the splendour and beauty of their flowers, their smell taste and figure, giv[ing] a kind of dignity to the vegetable community." Things get bloodier in the animal kingdom, as insects devour plants, birds devour insects, cats devour birds, and so up the ladder of size and ferocity until it's up to humans, "the last and highest minister of Nature," to keep the biggest, hungriest animals like whales in check. But all is for the best in this best of all possible worlds, according to Linnaeus's providential scheme. Every species is fortunately kept in check by another one; and in the "well regulated state" of nature, each species has its "proper employment and subsistence," just as the artisans and tradesmen of Paris do.[9] Diversity creates order.

Despite the mayhem of eating and being eaten at the local level, Linnaeus's economy of nature is stable and unchanging at the global level. Nature's well-regulated polity permits—indeed, depends on—the constant destruction of individuals in order to guarantee the preservation of the species, all of them. The order of nature was the order created by God, once and for all. Linnaeus did not countenance extinction. But the British lawyer and geologist Charles Lyell, writing in 1831 in the wake of spectacular discoveries of the fossil bones of animals like the giant sloth in South America or the mastodon in North America, brilliantly reconstructed by the comparative anatomist Georges Cuvier, could no longer deny the evidence that species that had once stalked the earth eons ago had since disappeared. Species, like individuals, must ultimately perish in consequence of both gradual and sudden changes in their habitats. Lyell nonetheless attempted to salvage Linnaeus's stable economy of nature by converting it into a steady-state one. When one species vacated its habitat, or simply dwindled in numbers, another rushed in to fill its place, an "invasion" (Lyell's term) facilitated by the broad geographic dispersion of many species. For Lyell, the Creator's wisdom manifested itself in exactly the kind of unchecked spread of species that Linnaeus had found so potentially fatal to nature's neat household, in which everything ideally had its place and stayed there. On the contrary, Lyell insisted, if "the Author Nature had not been so prodigal of those numerous contrivances" for dispersion and arranged that "the fluctuations of animate and inanimate creation should be in perfect harmony," then great gashes would open up in the economy of nature, places barren of all life. Happily, invasive species rushed in to fill the void left by the extinction of other species, topping up nature's cornucopia of forms.

But Lyell admitted that over the very long term—he estimated about a million years—such invasions would be inadequate to counterbalance extinctions. How then to fill up the holes left in the economy of nature and to replenish nature's diversity? Lyell contemplated the possible appearance of new species, only immediately to table the hypothesis until future generations of naturalists might turn up more evidence one way or another.[10] Accustomed as a geologist to thinking in terms of vast tranches of time, Lyell perhaps imagined a postponement of answers to such questions for at least a few centuries. But it took only about twenty-five years for his friend and protegé Charles Darwin to rush in where his mentor had feared to tread.

Darwin read both Linnaeus and Lyell on nature's economy, and although he clung to the metaphor and to the insight of a division of labor among species inhabiting different stations, just as workers in a metropolis like Paris ply different trades and professions, he destroyed all associations of diversity with stability and harmony, much less with divine providence. For Darwin, the diversity of organic life was not the *cause* of nature's economy but rather its *effect*. Like Linnaeus, he noted the tendency of each species to proliferate wildly if unchecked, and, like Lyell, he observed the tendency of species to disperse far and wide if unchecked. But instead of assuming that the existence and diversity of other species supplied the checks, each with its own station in nature's economy, Darwin explained the fact of diversity as the result of relentless competition among species for the *same* stations, now implicitly assumed to be a scarce resource, just as Thomas Malthus, also on Darwin's reading list in the 1830s, had assumed that the scarcity of the means of subsistence relative to the increase of the human population. In a memora-

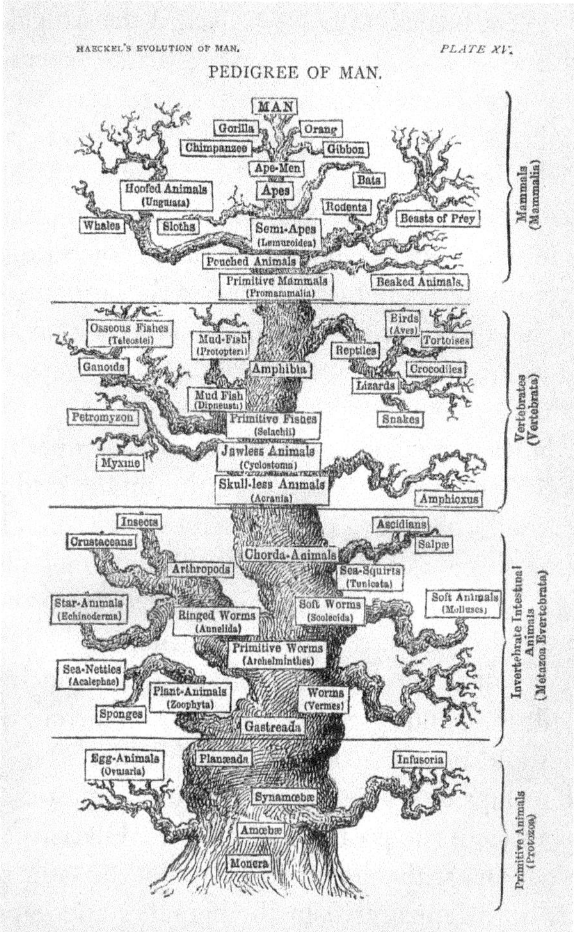

Fig. 2.5: Tree of Life. Source: Ernst Haeckel, *The Evolution of Man* (1879).

bly violent metaphor, Darwin likened the struggle of each species to increase its numbers at the expense of the others to "ten thousand sharp wedges packed close together and driven inwards by incessant blows" into the yielding "face of Nature."[11] In Darwin's notebook entry of September 28, 1838, it is 100,000 wedges bearing into not the face but "the economy of Nature."[12] To return to the division of labor in the human economy, it would be as if Parisian cobblers took up arms against neighboring candlemakers, who in turn invaded the shops of the milliners.

Under these circumstances of brutal competition, a variation that conferred even the slightest advantage might become a new branch on the tree of life, to revert to one of Darwin's more pleasant metaphors (Fig. 2.5). Instead of Linnaeus's noble trees protecting other organisms under their canopies, Darwin's tree is full of sprouting twigs trying to "branch out on all sides, and to overtop and kill the surrounding twigs and branches, in the same manner as species and groups of species have tried to overmaster other species in the great battle for life." Diversity and extinction are therefore two aspects of the same process, both represented in the branches and gaps of Darwin's one-and-only diagram (Fig. 2.1), which becomes "the great Tree of Life … cover[ing] the surface [of the earth] with its ever branching and beautiful ramifications."[13]

In this passage, as in the rhapsodic final lines of the *Origin of Species*, Darwin sugarcoats the murderous competition of those ten-thousand wedges and overmastering tree branches with the consolation of beauty. Yet the ultimate conclusion of his theory of evolution through natural selection was to reduce all beauty to utility. We human onlookers may marvel at those "endless forms most beautiful and most wonderful," but they are not meant for our admiration. *Pace* Linnaeus and Lyell, there is no divine artificer to craft and regulate nature's economy by an exquisite division of labor among species. *Pace* Pliny, the extravagant diversity of flowers shows nature hard at work, not at play. Darwin does still invoke Nature, always capitalized and often referred to by feminine pronouns, and his occasionally anthropomorphic turns of phrase to describe Nature's workings, especially in the parallels drawn between artificial and natural selection, made even some of his closest allies uneasy. The ghost of a benevolent deity haunts Darwin's account of natural selection: "Man selects only for his own good; Nature only for that of the being she tends."[14] But Darwin's nature was a flinty-eyed economist in the Victorian tradition, ruthlessly efficient and unflinchingly utilitarian. Darwin's nature scorned excess, was blind to beauty, and never took a day off. As if to bury Pliny's playful, spendthrift nature once and for all, Darwin devoted an entire monograph to showing that the most diverse and diversely beautiful of flowers were in fact ingeniously adapted to boost their chances in the struggle for life.

Flowers Go Baroque: The Case of Orchids

The botanical family of *Orchidaceae*, composed almost entirely of orchids, contains some 700 genera and 28,000 recognized species. Compare that to the family *Rosaceae*, which includes not only roses but many fruit-bearing plants such as apples, pears, plums, cherries, and strawberries, but has only 91 genera and a little under 5,000 species. Orchids are to flowers what baroque is to architectural styles: an over-the-top extravaganza of frills, flourishes, and frou-frou. To Darwin, orchids must have seemed a gauntlet thrown down to his claim that organic diversity was in fact a matter of utility and efficiency. What could possibly be the use of all those gaudy colors and multifarious forms of orchids? He therefore set out to show in detail almost as fulsome as the orchids themselves that all this apparently superfluous diversity served some purpose that promoted orchid survival. Even the most convoluted flowers and their parts revealed themselves on closer examination to be, in Darwin's words, "nu-

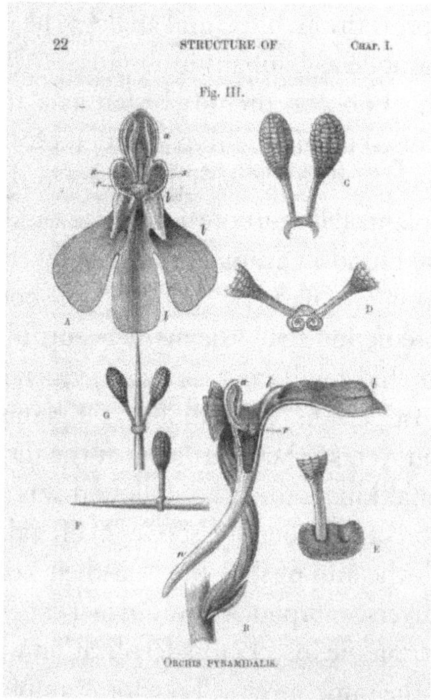

Fig. 2.6: G.B. Sowerby, *Structure of Orchis pyramidalis*. Source: Charles Darwin, *On the Various Contrivances by which British and Foreign Orchids Are Fertilised by Insects* (1862), Fig. III, p. 22.

merous and beautiful … contrivances" to avoid self-fertilization. Whenever he encountered what seemed at first glance to be a flagrantly useless form, Darwin doubled down. He asked, "How does Nature act?"—and the answer was always, by fitting form to function.[15] To press the architectural analogy, he set out to unmask baroque as Bauhaus in disguise.

Darwin's book on orchids began as a riposte to those botanists, including his good friend Joseph Dalton Hooker (1817–1911), who had claimed that adaptations in plants fell short of the intricacy and ingenuity of those found in animals and thereby cast doubt on the workings of natural selection.[16] The book opens with the prediction that "the many beautiful contrivances [of orchids] will exalt the whole vegetable kingdom in most persons' estimation," as if plants needed a champion to take their part against the more glamorous animal kingdom. What followed was a minute examination of one domestic species of orchid after another, with the aim of showing that their bizarre and bizarrely diverse morphology was in fact expertly engineered to promote insect cross-fertilization with other flowers of the same species. Take for example the *Orchis pyramidalis*, which Darwin praised for the "perfect adaptation" of its parts to coax the moths that feed on its nectar to spend a long time doing so, to make sure that they carry a maximum amount of pollen with them when they flit to the next flower (Fig. 2.6). Moths are attracted to the flower by its bright purple color by day and its scent by night; the long, narrow nectary fits the moth's proboscis like a kid glove and forces the moth to suck slowly; while the moth sucks the nectar, the viscous pollen it picks up has time to harden so that it won't shake off in flight; two flaps surrounding the moth's proboscis clasp it to insure it comes into contact with the pollen, "like a trap placed in a run for game." Darwin oscillates between meticulously detailed descriptions and exclamations of delight at the cleverness of what he repeatedly calls the orchid's "contrivances," a word redolent of fine craftsmanship.[17]

As he dissected orchid after orchid, often mimicking the action of insects with a fine bristle or a finger inserted into the flower, Darwin hammered home the message that even the strangest orchid shapes have some purpose in preventing the self-fertilization that he believed would reduce the fitness of offspring. Over and over again, he asked, what could be the use of some puzzling bit of orchid morphology? That it had no use was a possibility Darwin refused to countenance. When, for example, he encountered apparent barriers to flower fertilization in the hothouse orchids of the tribe *Vendeae*, of which Darwin examined twenty-nine genera, he confessed to perplexity as to "what purpose these qualities could serve." But Darwin's conviction that they must serve *some* purpose never wavered for a moment. In this case, he concluded that if an insect exited the flower at right angles, what at first appeared a hindrance could be a help in making the pollen stick.[18]

Occasionally, Darwin paused to mock the botanists who would explain away residual flower organs as specially created to round out the scheme of nature, and he took the immense variation among orchids to be counter-evidence to the Linnaean practice of finding "ideal types." Evolution through natural selection would, he was certain, soon replace such quaint aesthetic explanations with solid explanations based on common ancestors and homologies. In the conclusion to the book, Darwin trumpeted the victory of utility over "mere variety and beauty" even among the famously diverse and diversely beautiful family of orchids. Utility had carried the day: every "trifling detail of structure" has its use, as natural selection would lead one to expect.[19] As far as Darwin was concerned, baroque had been unmasked as Bauhaus.

Yet Darwin himself was alive to the beauty of orchids, or rather, to two competing kinds of beauty. Late in his treatise he ruminated on the question of which orchid represents the "highest" exemplar of the family. Should the laurels go to the *Ophreae*[20] or the showier *Vendiae*? Darwin hesitated. Should it be the *Ophreae*, whose structures had been most dramatically modified and therefore represented the cutting edge of evolution? Or should it be the gorgeous *Vendiae*, whose size, beautiful flower, and complex structure commanded universal admiration? Like Paris forced to judge the beauty contest between the goddesses Hera, Athena, and

Aphrodite in the ancient Greek myth, Darwin vacillated between his own strictly evolutionary standard of ever more efficient adaptation (Athena) and seductive aesthetic attractions (Aphrodite).

> [N]othing can be more perfect than the contrivances in Orchis pyramidalis for its fertilization. Yet an ill-defined feeling tells me to rank the magnificent Vendeae the highest.[21]

Just as in the myth, Aphrodite wins in the end.

The Problem of Useless Beauty

Neither Darwin nor his successors quite succeeded in laying the ghost of Pliny's useless beauty to rest. In a letter to the American botanist Asa Gray in April 1860, when hostile reviews the *Origin of Species* were preoccupying Darwin, he wrote that he was now confident that natural selection could account for the evolution of the eye, long the crown jewel of natural theology and the argument from divine design. But, as he confided to Gray, "now small trifling structures often make me very uncomfortable. The sight of a feather in a peacock's tail, whenever I gaze at it, makes me sick!"[22] The peacock's tail has since become emblematic of the problem of elaborate ornament—or even "small trifling structures"—with no apparent utility to the organism and therefore inexplicable by natural selection. Examples piled up in the annals of natural history and in Darwin's notes and correspondence: the remarkable plumage of the argus pheasant; the rococo nests of the Bower birds decorated with shells and feathers; the arias of the nightingale. Like the peacock's tail, these showy excesses not only gave the organism no advantage in the struggle for life; they also involved immense expenditure of energy, effort, and sometimes risk. The peacock who dragged a long tail behind him was far less likely to be able to hide from or to evade a predator. Such displays of beauty were worse than useless; they were expensive, even dangerous. Viewed from this perspective, it looked as if nature, ordinarily so frugal and briskly efficient, had gone on a wild spending spree.

For Darwin, the problem became so pressing that he introduced a second mechanism, sexual selection, to account for these anomalies, above the protests of some of his strongest supporters.[23] Pointing to the phenomenon of sexual dimorphism, in which the male and female of a species differ significantly in appearance, Darwin observed that it was usually the male who boasted brighter colors, striking excrescences like crests and antlers, or, in the case of birds, more complex song repertoires—all consistently displayed or deployed during mating season. In his 1871 treatise on sexual selection, Darwin heaped up examples of mostly male "ornaments," many from birds, which he pronounced to be "the most aesthetic of animals": the ruff of feathers around the neck of the British Ruff bird; a bullfinch who learned to sing a German waltz; the elegant ear-tufts of the pheasant; and of course the peacock's tail.[24] The diversity of these decorations concocted by nature beggared the human imagination—and enchanted the human observer's own sense of the beautiful. Darwin several times pointed out that gaily colored bird feathers ornamented many a lady's hat, proof positive that not only female birds found them attractive.

Although Darwin could not actually prove that the decorations, dances, and songs appealed to the females' aesthetic sensibility, he refused to accept the alternative: "If female birds had been incapable of appreciating the beautiful colours, the ornaments, and voices of their male partners, all the labour and anxiety exhibited by them in displaying their charms before the females would have been thrown away; and this it is impossible to admit."[25] Darwin was willing to countenance a role for beauty in evolution, at least beauty as judged by picky females making their choice among bower bird nests or fan-tailed peacocks. Such extravagances would then have a purpose, however circuitously fulfilled: to increase the male's reproductive fitness.

But what Darwin could not accept was extravagance and excess for its own sake, Pliny's nature at play.

The battle between utility versus beauty is still raging among evolutionary biologists.[26] On the side of utility, the latest explanation of the Darwin's "decorations" is the so-called "good gene" hypothesis.[27] To return once again to the splendid but costly peacock's tail that had so unsettled Darwin, the faction of utility argues that a glossy, iridescent tail "signals" low parasite load and general robustness to the peahen, who prudently chooses her mate on the basis of this proof of vigor, not beauty. Or alternatively, the tail is such a handicap that if the peacock has managed to survive until mating age, he must be extremely robust in all other respects. No aesthetic discernment need be attributed to the female, only a keen eye for signs of overall fitness that might be passed on to offspring. On the side of beauty, proponents emphasize the sophistication of animal perceptual systems and the anthropocentric awkwardness of reserving a sense of beauty for humans only.[28] I have no intention of adjudicating an ongoing debate. For my purposes, it suffices to point out that it *is* an ongoing debate: whether some of the most spectacular displays of diversity in the organic world are ultimately a matter of utility or of beauty—or both, as Darwin thought—is at bottom a battle between two versions of the value of diversity.

Conclusion: What to Do with Wonder?

Biodiversity has always evoked wonder among those who contemplate it, from Aristotle to today's visitors to natural history museums. It has also evoked admiration, wonder's boon companion, still fossilized in the Latin (and Romance language) words for wonder, *admiratio*. Beholders of early modern *Wunderkammern* exclaimed in both wonder and admiration for the extraordinary works of art and nature displayed ceiling-to-floor in glorious disregard for any ordering principle except plenitude and diversity. Many of the objects on display, such as seashells embellished with goldwork or scenes painted on landscape marble, deliberately blurred the distinction between nature and art: each vied with the other in a rivalrous collaboration between nature and the virtuoso craftsman. The image of nature as artificer, hammering out species at her forge, is very old, and it still survives in Darwin's admiration for nature's myriad "contrivances," even after he had tried to purge natural history of every trace of natural theology. For those steeped in the eighteenth-century tradition of natural theology, who pursued natural history as the glorification of God through the study of His works, wonder and admiration for biodiversity was a pious duty.

But it was also a delicious pleasure, a pleasure nourished by variety. Linnaeus went so far as to claim that variety was the "royal road" by which human beings traveled from an appreciation of nature to awed admiration for its creator. Variety was the tonic that stimulated the sated appetite and that relieved the mind of its cares. Without variety, habit would render us indifferent to the marvels of nature; wonder would wither and admiration stale. It was the variety of nature's works that stoked curiosity and opened our eyes not only to the beauty of flowers, but also to "their admirable structure, their odor, and their color." Diversity stimulated curiosity, and curiosity renewed wonder.[29] Darwin, enthralled by his orchids, would surely have agreed.

Yet no one did more than Darwin to block what for Linnaeus was almost a reflex, which connected wonder at nature's variety with admiration for divine workmanship. Darwin's correspondence and publications teem with exclamations of wonder for everything from barnacles to pheasants. But it is a truncated wonder, bereft of admiration, for there is no longer anyone to admire. Strictly speaking, the "endless forms most beautiful and most wonderful" are the result of chance variations acted upon necessary laws. Darwin was susceptible to the beauty of a tropical South American landscape or the feathers of the argus pheasant, but he reserved his greatest wonder—and admiration—

for what he repeatedly called "contrivances": intricate adaptations that solved evolutionary problems, like the exquisitely calibrated mechanisms by which various species of orchid prevented self-fertilization. But, as Darwin knew better than anyone, all those "ingenious contrivances" were not actually contrived. They merely happened, in a stumble-blunder process that unfolded over millions of years. Darwin was left with workmanship without the workman, and therefore with wonder without admiration. Perhaps this is one reason he was sometimes accused of personifying nature and turning natural selection into a semi-deity. Wonder without admiration is truncated wonder.

On at least one point Darwin and Linnaeus were in four-square agreement: variety is fundamental to the sense of beauty, both in humans and in other organisms. Darwin spent pages documenting the wildly divergent human standards of beauty in different cultures: some esteem beards and others abhor them; some prefer aquiline noses and others flat ones; smooth skin is admired by some, while others deliberately scarred their cheeks; and all peoples are convinced that their own skin color is the most beautiful and the others hideous. He concluded that there exists no absolute standard of beauty among humans; the most he would concede was the possible existence of an inherited taste for "brilliant colours and certain forms." Yet he did uphold one universal: everyone, everywhere likes variety. "If all our women were to become as beautiful as Venus de Medici, we should for a time be charmed; but we should soon wish for variety."[30] Despite his disagreement with Pliny on almost every other point, Darwin here echoes the ancient Roman naturalist: perhaps we, like Pliny's playful nature, like diversity for its own sake.

Chapter Three

Diversity as a Political Value

Introduction: What Kind of Value is Diversity?

The speed with which diversity has established itself as a social, political, and moral value must be baffling for many champions of the kindred value of equality. From Jean-Jacques Rousseau (1712–1778) to Mary Wollstonecraft (1759–1797) to Frederick Douglass (1818–1895) to John Rawls (1921–2002), the philosophers of equality have based their arguments on what is common to all human beings, not on what distinguishes one person from another. For Rousseau, harkening back to the Roman tradition of natural law, equality was the natural condition into which all human beings are born, just as animals are. For Mary Wollstonecraft, the equality of women was a matter of recognizing their full humanity as reasonable adults, not perpetual wards of their fathers, brothers, and husbands. The masthead motto of Dou-

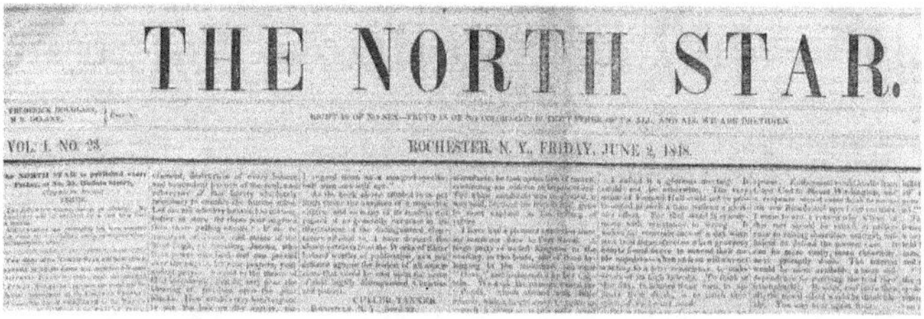
THE NORTH STAR.

VOL. I. NO. 23.

ROCHESTER, N. Y., FRIDAY, JUNE 2, 1848.

Fig. 3.1: Masthead motto of Frederick Douglass, *The North Star* (1848). Source: US Library of Congress.

glass's anti-slavery weekly *The North Star* was "Right is of no sex, Truth is of no color, God is the Father of us all, and all we are Brethren" (Fig. 3.1). Rawls' "veil of ignorance" thought experiment deliberately stripped human beings down to their most basic humanity and made justice blind to all specifics of identity. Even the sharpest critics of Enlightenment universalism as nothing more than bourgeois hypocrisy, like Karl Marx and Friedrich Engels, dreamt of a society without distinctions of wealth and privilege. How then did diversity, a vision of justice that celebrates distinctions of all kinds, displace equality, a vision of justice that deliberately ignores all such distinctions between noble and commoner, rich and poor, white and black, man and woman?

And why did this change take place so quickly? The struggle to entrench equality as a core value, a moral intuition that no longer needed to be argued for, has been

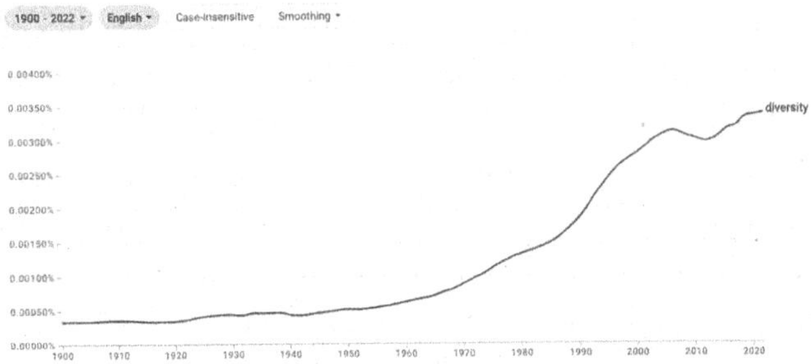

Fig. 3.2: Google N-Gram "Diversity" (1900-2020).

fought for centuries and is still not won. Even democracies founded on the principle of political equality are still riven by inequalities of wealth, health, education, and opportunity—inequalities that are widely tolerated and even taken for granted. The value of equality has evidently yet to become self-evident. In contrast, the value of diversity sems to have achieved that status in a matter of mere decades. Whatever criticisms have been leveled at heavy-handed efforts to institutionalize the value of diversity, such as Diversity-Equity-Inclusion (DEI) programs at corporations and universities, the intuition that a diverse society is a better society is strongly and sincerely felt, especially but not exclusively by younger people.

This Google Ngram is a crude but suggestive indicator of when the meteoric rise of diversity as a social, political, and moral value began (Fig. 3.2). (The fact that

I must use a three-headed modifier—"social, political, and moral"—to describe this value is partly because all norms of justice straddle these realms, but also partly because of the ambiguities inherent in the meaning of diversity, a point that I will return to later.) Starting circa 1970, the frequency with which the word appears in the Google Books corpus rises, but a closer look at the book titles from which the data base draws its sample suggests that the majority of these are about biodiversity, with a smaller number devoted to cultural diversity. After 1990, the rise is steeper, with a few small dips after 2010 but still at roughly five times the 1960 frequency. The titles of the books in the Google database shift decisively toward titles like *Encyclopedia of Diversity in Education* and *Managing Cultural Diversity,* although biodiversity is still prominently represented. If you search for the frequency of the word "equality" in

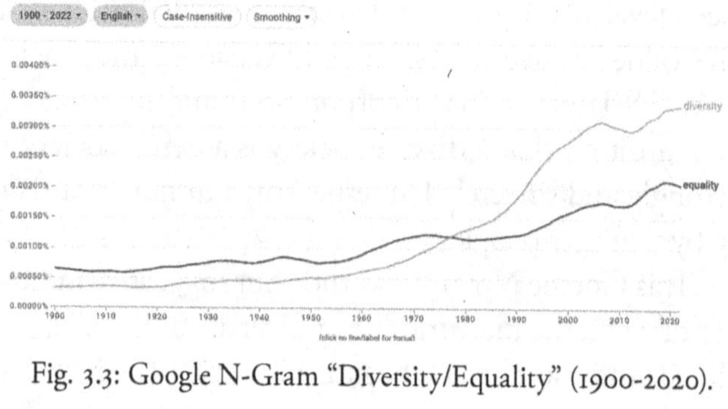

Fig. 3.3: Google N-Gram "Diversity/Equality" (1900-2020).

the same period, you also get a rising curve, but with a shallower slope and, more surprisingly, absolute values of use frequency that never achieve the highpoint of diversity (Fig. 3.3). I must once again caution that this is an indicator that should be used with a liberal shake of salt. Frequency of use does not necessarily imply approval or acceptance, and mere frequency yields no information about context and significance. But the results are nonetheless suggestive, especially when compared with cognate terms in other languages represented in the Google corpus. Both the shape of the curve and the dates of the inflection points tally, with about a five-year lag time, with results for *diversité* in French and *Diversität* in German—albeit with sharper dips around 2010. These results suggest at least a rough periodization and also the direction of influence from the US to Europe, as in the German case, in which "diversity" begins as an English import, showing a steep rise between 2000 and 2010, and then is naturalized thereafter as *Diversität*, which latter term has increased in frequency of usage inexorably ever since.

Because these developments are still ongoing, this chapter cannot unknot the tangle of circumstances that led to the apparently irresistible rise of diversity as a value of justice, much less to still raging controversies over the policies designed to realize that value. Moreover, by its very nature, the advent of diversity as a political value is a story that has unfolded differently in different historical and cultural contexts. The kind of diversity that matters in Germany or Austria sometimes diverges sharply from versions in the US, the UK, and France, not to mention in India or Brazil, for example. Whether race, religion, national origin, ethnicity, language, or sexuality dominates the political debate about diversity depends on past history and present politics. This is still a story that is unfolding as I write, and it would be reckless for any historian to pronounce upon the present, much less upon the future. What a historical perspective can provide is insight into how diversity became a political value at all—and why it did so with breathtaking speed. I will therefore focus on the moment when diversity began its alpine rise as a value of justice, in the period before about 2000. My thesis is that its appeal over older, universalist values of equality owed much to diversity's earlier career, first as a value of aesthetics and later also as a value of economics, the subjects of chapters 1 and 2. In this chapter, I will argue that diversity never severed its kinship ties with beauty and efficiency, and that these already entrenched values accelerated its acceptance in the social, political, and moral realms.

Although the crystallization of diversity as justice is a recent phenomenon, the tension between diversity and universalism in the political realm goes back to the Enlightenment, which is where I will begin as well. My story then fast-forwards to the mid-twentieth century and to the political developments that first introduced the value of diversity as a form of justice. This latest incarnation of the value of diversity piggy-backed on the symbols of diversity as beauty and the arguments for diversity as efficiency to vaunt the virtues of diversity as justice. But it is in the nature of diversity to be diverse, and very soon fault lines began to open up among factions battling to be included in the definition of diversity as justice. I will conclude with some brief reflections on the problem with which I began this book: what does this history of the shape-shifting value of diversity teach us about the nature of value per se? And which side is winning the Enlightenment quarrel between diversity and universalism?

The Enlightenment vs. the Enlightenment

The quarrel between diversity and universalism pitted the Enlightenment against itself. Star *philosophes* like the Baron de Montesquieu (1689–1755) and the Marquis de Condorcet (1743–1794) squared off against each other. Montesquieu's *De l'Esprit des lois* (1748) famously argued that the diversity of climates and topographies created a diversity of cultures exquisitely attuned to their surroundings and that legislators should respect that diversity in matching laws to cultures. The idea was as old as Herodotus's observation that in Egypt everything was topsy-turvy by ancient Greek standards, both nature and culture: just as the Nile flowed south to north in contrast to Greek rivers that flowed north to south, so Egyptian men stayed home and wove at their looms while women went out to the market to truck and barter.[1] Montesquieu's book caused a sensation by mustering a dazzling display of comparative legal examples from both ancient and modern, European and non-European cultures to sharpen his point—and then aiming this barbed weapon against the efforts of the French crown to standardize regional customs into centralized, uniform law for the entire kingdom. Montesquieu buttressed his arguments about ineradicable cultural diversity with claims about natural diversity—not just the diversity of climates but also of physiology. How could one expect the peoples of Spain, made highly excitable and irritable by the hot climate that dilated their nerve endings, to follow the same laws as the phlegmatic Germans and Dutch, whose cold climate contracted their nerves to the point that they had to get drunk as skunks in order to feel anything at all?[2]

Montesquieu was much admired for his liberal principles during the Enlightenment, especially his doctrine of the separation of powers and his opposition to the overweening ambitions of absolute monarchs. But

Condorcet, another passionate Enlightenment liberal, took vehement exception to what he regarded as Montesquieu's attack on universal natural rights. In his commentary on the twenty-ninth book of *De l'Esprit des lois*, in which Montesquieu had argued, among other things, that the very same law that had been good in ancient Rome was nonetheless bad in modern France, Condorcet threw down the gauntlet:

> Because truth, reason, justice, the rights of man, property interests, liberty, [and] security are the same everywhere, all provinces of a state or even all states should have the same criminal, civil, and commercial laws. A good law should be good for everyone, just as a true proposition is true for all.[3]

Just as Montesquieu had propped up his defense of legal diversity by appeal to the diversity of natural habitats, from the sub-tropical Mediterranean to the vast Asian plains or North American forests, Condorcet defended legal universality in the name of natural law, defined in Roman law as that which human beings share with animals, and elevated by early modern jurists such a Hugo Grotius (1583–1645) and Samuel Pufendorf (1632–1694) to the status of the foundation of all law, for all peoples. Depending on which nature one chose to emphasize, the patchwork ecosystems of natural history or the stately regularities of celestial mechanics, nature could be enlisted on either side of the Enlightenment quarrel between diversity and universalism. But the debate was never really about the facts of nature or even human nature; it was about the clashing values of diversity and universalism.

This Enlightenment background should be kept in mind as we now turn to more recent debates over diversity versus universalism. These debates are not new, despite enormous shifts in political context and in the meanings of diversity. Nor is the fact that these debates tend to pit liberals against each other, rather than against reactionaries, a modern novelty. Both Montesquieu and Condorcet represented the progressive wing of Enlightenment political thought; their quarrel was an internal one among the party of reform about how an improved society should be governed. Like the party of reform today, they were convinced that their society was unjust and that reforms were urgently needed. Their differences are in part still our differences, even if we long ago stopped wearing powdered periwigs and writing with quill pens.

From Equality to Diversity

There are distinct echoes of the Enlightenment debate in the more recent debates about whether the values of equality and diversity really promote the same vision of justice. There is widespread agreement among scholars that the rise and rise of diversity as a political value began in the United States in the 1960s with campaigns for equality, first and foremost the Civil Rights movement to secure equal rights for black Americans. In campaigns closely modeled on the Civil Rights movement, activist groups representing first women, and later gays and lesbians organized to tear down legal barriers to equality, especially in the job and housing market. All three of these movements marched under the banner of equality for all citizens, regardless of race, gender, or sexuali-

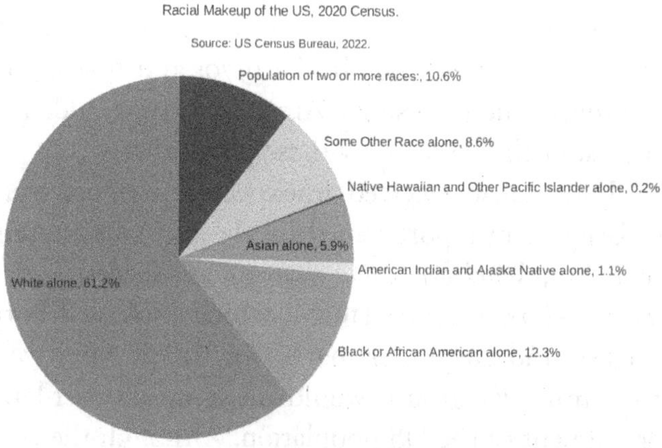

Fig. 3.4: Racial Makeup of the United States.
Source: US Census 2020.

ty, and all three fortified their claims to equal treatment in a democracy with demographic arguments: how could a significant portion of the population (estimates as to percentages comprised by each group varied from 10 percent to 50 percent) be denied equal rights? Accordingly, legislation and government programs that attempted to redress these wrongs, such as Equal Employment Opportunity and Affirmative Action, set goals for each of these groups in the workplace, the military, the civil service, and the universities that matched their statistical proportion of the population.[4] (Fig. 3.4) For example, if black Americans represented 12 percent of the population, then they should ideally constitute 12 percent of public sector employees, university students, army officers, business executives, etc. In the 1970s and 1980s, other groups, such as Native Americans, were added to the list of those served by these programs.

Their cause received unexpected support from a Reagan era report issued by the US Department of Labor, *Workforce 2000: Work and Workers for the Twenty-First Century* (1987), which projected both a labor and consumer market in which what were then minority groups would make up an ever-larger segment of the US population. Although the conservative Reagan government and an even more conservative Supreme Court generally sought to cut back

Affirmative Action and Equal Employment Opportunity programs, the Department of Labor report spurred American businesses to rethink their hiring practices in preparation for this predicted demographic shift. This was also the moment when many US firms began courting global markets, and there were obvious advantages to hiring employees from immigrant backgrounds who spoke the languages of billions of non-American consumers worldwide. Unlike the programs that had resulted from political campaigns for equality, these policy changes among businesses were driven by profit motivation. Especially after a number of landmark Supreme Court decisions struck down Affirmative Action programs as unconstitutional, a new specialty known as "diversity management" replaced Affirmative Action offices in both the public and private sectors. In the US, "diversity" had decisively edged out "equality" in policies and mission statements by the 1990s; by 2012, the European Union had also begun to adopt the language of "diversity" in its directives to member states. European countries with strong corporate ties to the US, such as Germany, were in the vanguard of adopting both the new language and new measures.[5]

The rise of diversity correlated with the decline of equality, the latter understood as the proportional representation of groups that had been historically the victims of discrimination—mostly ethnic minorities, but also women, who were by most counts the majority of the population. At this point in the story, the spotlight shifts from government and business to the university. The pivotal event was the US Supreme Court decision in the case of *Bakke v. Regents of the University of California* (438 US 285 (1978)) in 1978. Allan Bakke's application to the University of California, Davis medical school had been twice rejected, and Bakke, a thirty-five-year-old white man, sued the university for violation of his right to equal protection under the law, as guaranteed by the Fourteenth Amendment to the US Constitution, because he believed that the university's affirmative action policies discriminated in favor of black applicants at the expense of white applicants like himself. The majority opinion of the Supreme Court struck down the university's policy of reserving a certain number of places in each medical school class for black students as unconstitutional, but upheld the university's right to take race into account as one dimension among many in the evaluation of applicants in the interests of promoting "diversity." Writing for the majority, Justice Lewis Powell cited with approval Harvard University's recently enlarged "concept of diversity to include students from disadvantaged economic, racial and ethnic groups." Powell went on to provide a vivid example:

> When the [Harvard] Committee on Admissions reviews the large middle group who are 'admissible' and deemed capable of doing good work in their courses, the race of an applicant may tip the balance in his favor just as geographic origin or a life spent on a farm may tip the balance in other candidates' cases. A farm boy from Idaho can bring something to Harvard College that a Bostonian cannot offer. Similarly, a black student can usually bring something that a white person cannot offer ....[6]

Harvard had in fact had a long policy of deliberately diversifying its student body, dating back to before the Civil War, but justified in terms not of equality or diversity but of the free marketplace of ideas propounded by nineteenth-century liberals like John Stuart Mill: if students from the North and South were allowed to debate their conflicting views about slavery face-to-face, in a gentlemanly fashion, perhaps armed conflict might be averted—so the optimistic justification of Harvard's admission policies circa 1850. After World War II, Harvard's policy of diversification received another boost, but with an entirely different justification: Harvard president James Bryant Conant, a chemist and chief administrator of the atomic bomb project, want to admit more students solely on grounds of academic excellence—which in practice meant getting rid of the restrictive quotas for Jewish students.[7] During the Civil Rights era, Harvard again reinterpreted diversity to include black students and later women. The policy seems to have eventually produced the desired results, at least by some measures.

Almost overnight after the *Bakke* decision, the diversity argument replaced other justifications for positive discrimination in favor of disadvantaged minorities among universities in the United States, most notably the argument of a duty to undo the historical effects of slavery and prejudice and to compensate for structural economic and social inequalities. Astonishingly, the response to the *Bakke* decision was almost universally positive: the conservative right rejoiced in the fact that racial quotas had been eliminated (and that Allan Bakke had finally been admitted to medical school); the liberal left celebrated the diversity doctrine as the royal road to including minorities not only in elite universities like Harvard but also in the ranks of corporate executives and military officers. As the *Wall Street Journal* summed up prevailing reactions in its headline on the occasion of the Supreme Court decision, *Bakke* was a case that "everybody won." Not everyone was happy with the diversity solution: some liberal legal scholars complained that the elevation of diversity over equality obscured the claims of reparative justice for people who had suffered slavery, violence, and ongoing discrimination;[8] some conservative scholars argued that in order to qualify as a criterion in university admissions, diversity of race must be shown to be educationally relevant.[9] But until the current Supreme Court overturned the Bakke decision in 2023[10] (notably in a case filed against Harvard), diversity-as-inclusion was not only the law of the land; it was almost a moral platitude, as unassailable as motherhood and apple pie.[11]

I do not wish to exaggerate the influence of a single American court case. Other, arguably more momentous political events elsewhere in the world surely prepared the way for the astonishing success of diversity as a political value. Here I can only give one example, but one which attracted worldwide attention—not least at Harvard. After the first democratic elections of April 1994 that elected Nelson Mandela (1918–2013) to the presidency of South Africa, Archbishop Desmond Tutu (1931–2021) declared that South Africans were "the rainbow people of God. We are free—all of us, black and white together!" Tutu's rainbow was an explicitly religious symbol, meant to evoke the rainbow that sealed the covenant between God and humanity after the flood.[12] Mandela however adapted the phrase to more civic, secular ends and underscored the multiracial associations of the multicolored rainbow in his first presidential inaugural address in May 1994:

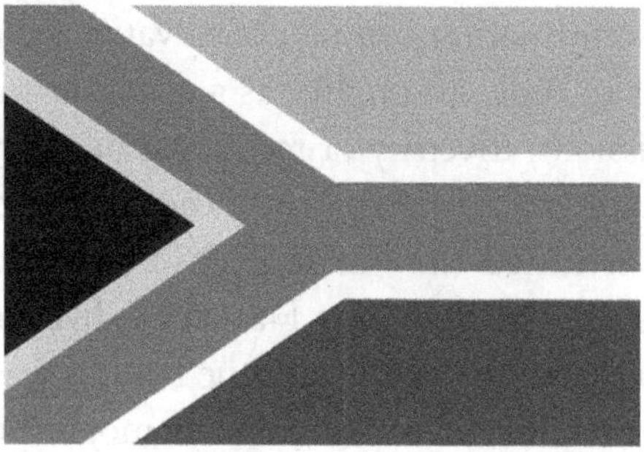

Fig. 3.5: South African Flag (adopted 1994).

"We enter into a covenant that we shall build the society in which all South Africans, both black and white, will be able to walk tall, … a rainbow nation at peace with itself and the world."[13] Even though South Africa rejected a rainbow motif for its new flag after an initial proposal, the design ultimately adopted in 1994 contains six colors (black, white, gold, red, blue, and green), more than any other flag, and almost immediately interpreted as representing a convergence of the country's diverse peoples.[14] (Fig. 3.5)

The American and South African parts of this story might not have been as unconnected as they seem at first glance. Once again, the missing link seems to have been Harvard. Even before the end of apartheid, some South African universities, notably the University of Cape Town and the University of Witwatersrand, had defended "racial diversity within the university" as fundamental to a multiracial society against the apartheid government. By a circuitous route, these arguments reached the ears of the Harvard Law School professors who drafted the brief that Justice Powell quoted with such approval in the *Bakke* decision. The chancellors of both South African universities, one of whom was also Chief Justice in that country, had visited Harvard Law School and left a deep impression on some of its faculty, some of whom went on to write influential briefs that framed the question of justice in terms of diversity, rather than equality or reparation.[15] Despite very different histories and politics, there were resonant chords struck between South Africa and the United States, two multiracial nations striving to heal the scars left by slavery, conquest, and segregation, and also two nations that had historically both defined race by skin color. By the end of the first decade of the twenty-first century, diversity had become a self-evident value in many countries, and its universal symbol became the rainbow, South Africa's proud badge of many colors.

Echoes of Diversity Past

But what kind of value did the rainbow really represent? The advocates of diversity portrayed it as justice achieved by the full inclusion of all members of society, an open-armed embrace of different identities—identities that had been solidified in the previous decades by many of the policies initially designed to redress historical inequalities. Political campaigns for the rights of women or Muslims or blacks cast individual identities in those molds. Checking boxes by race or gender or ethnicity on official forms designed to enforce first equal opportunity and later diversity cemented these identities further: statistical classification became self-classification.[16] These identities came to be perceived as indelible and also as immiscible as the distinct colors of the rainbow, a ubiquitous metaphor of diversity that replaced older metaphors of multicultural societies as a melting pot. Just as it would entirely destroy the beauty of the rainbow to mix red, yellow, orange, green, blue, indigo and violet into a murky gray, so it would destroy the vitality of a multicultural society to insist that all of its members blend into the bland, porridge-y uniformity of the melting pot. This version of diversity-as-justice emphasized high-spirited pageantry: diversity was to be celebrated (an oft-repeated verb) in parades and festivals. At these exuberant displays of diversity, inclusion was staged not only by the persons of the participants but also by a kaleidoscope of colorful costumes, banners, and floats.

It might be objected that these resonances between the ancient value of diversity-as-beauty and the brand-new value of diversity-as-justice are no more than mere imagery and metaphors. Imagery and metaphors they certainly are—that is how aesthetics works. But there is nothing "mere" about them. By visualizing diversity-as-justice as a festival of costumes and colors, proponents of an inclusive society tapped into the pleasing and peaceable spectacle of nature at play—the ancient Roman naturalist Pliny's explanation for the pointless profusion of the many kinds of flowers and gemstones, as we saw in chapter 1. These happy associations were particularly useful in political contexts in which an inclusive society meant bringing together groups that had only recently been in violent conflict with each other, as in post-apartheid South Africa. In one of his many rhetorical variations on the rainbow-nation theme, Mandela conjured images that eerily recalled Pliny's paean to the diversity of flowers:

> I have no hesitation in saying that each of us is as intimately attached to the soil of this beautiful country as are the famous jacaranda trees of Pretoria and the mimosa trees of the buschveld.[17]

For those familiar with South African flora, Mandela's analogies conjured up visions of avenues lined with jacaranda trees in spectacular lavender bloom and the golden splendor of a blossom-laden mimosa. Nestled in the heart of the political value of diversity-as-justice still lies the multi-colored splendor of the flowering meadow, diversity-as-beauty.

Diversity-as-efficiency also shadowed diversity-as-justice. In the ramifying applications of the arguments of the *Bakke* decision in realms as various as optimizing decisions in the workplace to fortifying scientific research against bias, the principle of the division of labor buttressed the value of diversity-as-inclusion. It was plausibly argued by sociologists, psychologists, and even philosophers of science that teams composed of people representing diverse standpoints, deriving from diverse identities and life experiences, were better at solving problems than more homogeneous groupings. Like the workers in the pin factory, or the organs of the body, each member of the diverse team was perceived to contribute something unique and essential to the success of the whole.

Businesses in both the US and Europe regarded what came to be called "diversity management" as a sterling example of doing well by doing good. They took the "doing good" part for granted: if diversity was indeed a value of justice, then it followed axiomatically that diversifying their work forces promoted justice—and incidentally burnished the public image of the firms that did so as good corporate citizens. But since businesses had to show profits in order to survive, the "doing well" part of the justification for diversity management carried more weight. Advocates for diversity argued that teams of employees from diverse backgrounds would bring diverse perspectives that would correct the biases and blind spots of more homogeneous groups and lead to more creative problem solving. Moreover, representatives of different groups—be they women, ethnic minorities, the disabled, or almost any other category other than the "white, male, middle-aged, able-bodied, heterosexual"—would, so the claim, possess different skills consonant with their different identities.[18] The resulting division of labor would theoretically increase efficiency and productivity. For example, in a globalized economy, employees from diverse ethnic backgrounds and language skills might help open up foreign markets. Finally, the company lawyers pointed out that compliance with diversity guidelines would be considerably cheaper than fighting expensive discrimination suits in court. For once, the dictates of profit and prudence seemed to align with those of conscience in this best of all possible worlds. By 1992, more than 75 percent of America's biggest companies had hired a diversity manager, and by 2010, many European companies had followed their example.[19]

Similar arguments emphasizing the division of labor as well as fairness were made on behalf of diversity in the realm of scientific research. But this time, the advertised benefits were epistemic rather than financial. During the 1970s and 1980s, researchers in the biomedical and behavioral sciences became increasingly uneasy about the stereotypical assumptions imbedded in much past research about racial and gender differences. Critically examined in light of the campaigns for political equality, many of these assumptions now seemed not just false but wrong. Were women really disqualified from high public office and other demanding careers because of hormonal imbalances?[20] Were black people really less intelligent than white people?[21] Was homosexuality really a mental illness?[22] All of these dubious claims, supported by still more dubious experiments, could be found in respectable scientific publications. Alarm bells started ringing among both scientists and the general public about whether scientists could be trusted to police their own biases. It was also glaringly obvious that the groups most affected by such claims were barely represented among the ranks of scientists. Like business, science stood exposed as a microcosm of an unjust society that had excluded many groups from full participation on no more than prejudice.

For philosophers of science, the problem was even more acute. Decades of reflection on science past and present had shown that empirical data never suffice on their own to generate explanatory hypotheses or to determine unambiguously the choice between rival theories. Beliefs and values therefore necessarily supplemented observation and experiment in order to make scientific progress possible. But whose beliefs and values? This was an especially tricky question in research involving human beings. If the scientist's own identity carried with it uncritical and damaging assumptions about other groups—and the historical record delivered abundant evidence that this had often been the case—then such beliefs and values could subvert the truth. Once again, arguments about the division of labor in scientific research fortified arguments for diversity among scientific researchers. If each individual's distinctive identity came with an equally distinctive perspective, then the different perspectives of a diverse research team would mutually correct each other's biases—or so the hope. For example, a team that included female as well as male scientists would be more likely to spot and to correct gender biases on both sides if such assumptions entered into the investigation. Objectivity would thereby be restored not by eliminating subjectivity in each and every scientist but rather by pitting one kind of subjectivity against another.[23]

This was the liberal solution to the scientists' dilemma. As in John Stuart Mill's free marketplace of ideas, truth was assumed to emerge victorious from the combat among conflicting perspectives, so long as the combat was conducted on an egalitarian basis according to fair rules of engagement. But there was a more radical version of the diversity solution, so-called standpoint epistemology, which privileged the perspectives of those researchers who belonged to oppressed groups, at least for certain objects of inquiry. Who could understand the patriarchy better than the women who suffered under it? Who could understand racism better than its victims? Proponents of standpoint epistemology also pointed out that identity influenced not only how scientific knowledge was acquired but also what that knowledge was about. Why was it, they asked, that publicly funded medical research disproportionately studied diseases that affected men rather than women?[24] Standpoint epistemologies doubled down on how identity defined perspective and asserted that some perspectives were epistemologically superior to others, not just counterweights to prevailing biases.[25] Both the liberal and radical versions of the argument for diversity-as-justice in science assumed that perspective followed inexorably from identity, and that identity was destiny.

But what was identity? This question bedeviled every attempt to put the ideal of diversity-as-justice into practice, whether in the office or the laboratory, the classroom or the boardroom. What began as a relatively short list of identities inherited from equal opportunity and affirmative action programs grew longer and longer as more and more groups laid claim to distinctive identities based on economic status, physical appearance, cognitive style, educational background, neurological constitution, regional origin, mother tongue, or simply lifestyle. As the value of diversity-as-justice spread to countries around the world, other dimensions of diversity were added to the list. For example, in several Central European countries, the Roma were historically salient as an excluded minority, whereas in France, Belgium, Britain, and the Netherlands, it was the descendants of immigrants from former colonies. In short, diversity is diverse, sometimes bitterly so. As anyone who has ever sat in a committee charged with implementing a diversity program knows, the competing claims of all these groups to recognition and prerogatives in no way resemble the good-natured festivals that celebrate diversity in street parades.

Nor have the hoped-for benefits of diversity in terms of productivity in business stood up to critical scrutiny. Several decades of academic research devoted to measuring the effects of diversity have failed to deliver a clearcut result—in part because each study defines diversity differently.[26] The verdict on diversity in science is mixed: the inclusion of women and minorities previously excluded as researchers has widened the focus of topics studied, most notably in biomedical fields.[27] Many of the most pointed criticisms of biases in previous research also come from researchers who are themselves members of the affected groups. Whether diversified research teams are more creative is more difficult to assess—once again, because criteria for creative science are variously and fuzzily defined and because of the many conflating factors.[28] Yet despite these problems, the value of diversity-as-justice has nonetheless taken swift and deep root in the garden of our moral intuitions. Standing on the shoulders of older values of diversity as beauty and efficiency, the irresistible rise of the value of diversity-as-inclusion is perhaps not so mysterious after all.

Conclusion: A Value Is a Value Is a Value

I began this book with a question: what kind of value is diversity? And what does the answer to that question teach us about the nature of value more generally? The answer that emerges from the long history that I've sketched in these three chapters is that diversity is not one but several values: a value of beauty, a value of efficiency, and a value of justice. These various normative valences are cumulative: in the nineteenth century, the value of efficiency was added to the ancient value of beauty, and in the late twentieth century, the value of justice was added to the long-established values of beauty and efficiency. As we have seen, this tripartite compound of beauty, efficiency, and justice was not entirely stable. In order to admire the beauty of biodiversity, even Darwin had to mute the brutally efficient competition that brought it about—those 10,000 wedges being hammered into the yielding face of nature. And in order to make justice pay, advocates of diversity in business and science had to make bold claims about efficiency and productivity gains that have yet to be cashed out.

Wherever the value of diversity was invoked—as beauty, efficiency, or justice—the problem of how much diversity was too much diversity had to be confronted. How much miscellany could even the famously miscellaneous *Wunderkammern* cram into every nook and cranny before degenerating into a junk heap? How finely could labor be divided before the overall task lost all coherence? How many dimensions of diversity had to be taken into account until the inclusive society dissolved into an aggregate of individual identities? Yet despite these flaws, the multiple values of diversity are still our values, and they mutually reinforce each other. To borrow a metaphor dear to proponents of diversity, a harmonic chord sounds louder and more melodious if played by the whole orchestra than just on a single instrument. Without the resonances with diversity as beauty and as efficiency, it is unlikely that diversity as justice would have advanced from intellectual position to visceral moral intuition in the space of barely a generation. Diversity is not one value but at least three—and apparently all the stronger for that.

Apparently. The past wanderings of the value of diversity do seem to have smoothed the way for its latest incarnation as a value of justice. But diversity's long history as a value of some kind did not necessarily fuse that value into a smooth monolith, without cracks or seams. On the contrary, very soon fault lines opened up between justice and beauty and between justice and efficiency. Some critics suspected diversity of being an agreeable aesthetic of difference expressed in consumer products—more "Benetton than Barricades," as some of them put it—and of thereby overlooking the still stark realities of racism.[29] Others pointed out that the dictates of ethics and efficiency in the workplace might not go hand-in-hand, might even tug in opposite directions.[30] Although these critics seemed unaware of the long and motley history of the value of diversity, they did spot the incoherences that were as much part of the legacy of that history as the meteoric rise of the most recent value of diversity-as-justice had been a few decades before. For better or for worse, the value of diversity has a history, and that history has consequences.

Does the history of the wandering value of diversity teach us anything about value in general? It would be rash to generalize from one example, however long-lived and widespread. Philosophers have long since abandoned the hope that the good, the true, and the beautiful might all turn out to be variants of the same thing, and modern philosophy has divided the territory of values into separate nations, each an island unto itself. There are the utilitarian values of efficiency and productivity, the aesthetic values of beauty and creativity, the epistemic values of truth and objectivity, and the ethical values of justice and inclusion. Officially, there is no traffic among these island nations; each recognizes only the currency of its own distinctive brand of value. At very least, the history of the wandering value of diversity ought to alert us to the fact that the boundaries between the realms of aesthetics and utility, ethics and epistemology are not watertight, and that there is some cross-border smuggling going on. Perhaps the history of the many faces of the value of diversity is an anomaly, albeit a striking and consequential one. If, however, there turn out to be other such cases of wandering values, then we might at least entertain the hypothesis that what we classify as different kinds of values, as different as the elements of gold, silver, and copper, may actually be more like a single fungible currency—to press a bit further the conceit of island nations, each with its own coinage. Value in one realm may confer value in another, however illegitimately from a strictly philosophical point of view. But then, we historians exist to remind the philosophers that there are more things in heaven and earth than have been heard of in their philosophy.

I began this chapter with one of the many episodes of the Enlightenment having it out with itself: Montesquieu versus Condorcet, diversity versus universalism. Who won? There is an irenic argument that claims that with the advent of diversity-as-justice, both sides won. Although diversity enjoys far better press these days than universalism does, their goals are said to largely converge. A fervent abolitionist and campaigner for women's rights, Condorcet understood his universalism as an open-armed embrace of all people in a worldwide community of equal rights and responsibilities.

Yet he might have balked at the idea of diversity being an intrinsic character of individuals, just as he balked at Montesquieu's claim that human cultures were indelibly and intrinsically diverse. Although no one would deny that the specifics of history and culture and of nature and nurture shape individual perspectives and identities, for Condorcet such traits were irrelevant to claims to full citizenship and indeed full humanity. Such peculiarities might enrich or impoverish a polity, but what qualified individuals for full participation as citizens was what they had in common: their reason and their humanity. Precisely those qualities made it possible to shift perspectives, to escape their own experience and assumptions and enter into those of other reasonable beings. The party of Montesquieu might mock Condorcet's obsessive concern with uniformity, not just of laws but also of weights and measures and house façades. Yet the uniformity of individuals with respect to their exercise of reason was fundamental to him in ways that sit uncomfortably with all versions of diversity as a value.

The modern party of Montesquieu challenges Condorcet's universalism as at best boring—how can bland uniformity compete with the colorful tapestry of human cultures and identities?—and at worst as self-deceived—universalism is either a fraud or a fantasy. But as yet, they have no answer to one last challenge from the party of Condorcet: don't all three versions of diversity as a value—as beauty, as efficiency, as justice—imprison us in our dappled identities? Just as the workers in Adam Smith's pin factory achieve efficiency at the price of narrow, repetitive specialization, and Pliny's flower-spangled meadows achieve their pied beauty by mingling fixed species, the identities combined in those collectives (college classes, workplace teams, scientific collaborations) forged by diversity-as-inclusion are assumed to be permanent and paramount—both our life's capital and our life's chains. Analogies between cultural diversity and biodiversity are rife, but that analogy comes at a cost.[31] Are our identities really like biological species? The result of mere chance and the shuffle of circumstance, our accidental identities trail us like shadows, always and everywhere. Within the framework of diversity, our perspectives are valuable because they are reliably generic—and also reliably rigid: the one woman who has been recruited to a committee is expected to represent that perspective, and no other. Diversity-as-justice rooted itself in our intuitions as a value in part because it drew upon earlier versions of diversity as an aesthetic and as an economic value. But that heritage also came with a tacit assumption that diversity was primarily a matter of combining stable kinds, specialized by task or ecological niche, not plastic individuals. Proverbially, the leopard cannot change its spots. Can we still change our perspectives and our identities?

Endnotes

All translations are my own unless otherwise specified.

Chapter One

[1] Hdt. 3.39 in Herodotus, *The History*, trans. David Grene (University of Chicago Press, 1987), 228; see Sally Humphreys, "Law, Custom and Culture in Herodotus," *Arethusa* 20, no. 1/2 (1987): 211–20, https://www.jstor.org/stable/44578858.

[2] Nathalie Heinich, "Framing the Bull Fight: Aesthetics versus Ethics," *British Journal of Aesthetics* 33, no. 1 (1993): 52–58, https://doi.org/10.1093/bjaesthetics/33.1.52.

[3] Plin. *HN.* Praef. in Pliny the Elder, *Natural History*, rev. ed., trans. H. Rackham, vol. 1 of 10, *Books 1–2*, Loeb Classical Library 330 (Harvard University Press, 1949), 12–13.

[4] Plin. *HN.* 21.1 in Pliny the Elder, *Natural History*, trans. W. H. S. Jones, vol. 6 of 10, *Books 20–23*, Loeb Classical Library 392 (Harvard University Press, 1951), 160–61.

[5] Plin. *HN.* 37.1, 37.12 in Pliny the Elder, *Natural History*, trans. D. E. Eichholz, vol. 10 of 10, *Books 36–37*, Loeb Classical Library 419 (Harvard University Press, 1962), 164–65, 200–203.

[6] Plin. *HN.* 37.1, 37.21 in Pliny, *Natural History*, 10:164–65, 228–29.

[7] The main medieval and early modern source for these properties of gemstones was book 17 of Bartholomeus Anglicus, *De genuinis rerum coelestium, terrarum et inferarum proprietatibus libri XVIII* (Frankfurt, 1601), 724, 732, 746, 748, which was first written ca. 1240. The most in-

fluential early modern lapidary was by Anselm de Boodt, physician to the Holy Roman Emperor Rudolph II: *Gemmarum et lapidum historia* (Leiden, 1647).

8 Robert Boyle, *An Essay About the Origine and Virtues of Gems* (London, 1672), 177–78. Bloodstones or heliotropes are usually mixtures of green chalcedony and red jasper.

9 Plin. *HN.* 21.1 in Pliny, *Natural History*, 6:160–61.

10 Francis Darwin, *The Life and Letters of Charles Darwin*, 3rd ed. (London, 1887), 2:296, but see Raghavendra Gadagkar, "Is the Peacock Merely Beautiful or Also Honest?," *Current Science* 85, no. 7 (2003): 1012–20, https://www.jstor.org/stable/24108784.

11 Immanuel Kant, *Kritik der Urteilskraft*, ed. Wilhelm Weischedel (Suhrkamp, 1974), § 4, p. 120.

12 A. J. Close, "Commonplace Theories of Art and Nature in Classical Antiquity and in the Renaissance," *Journal of the History of Ideas* 30, no. 4 (1969): 467–86, https://doi.org/10.2307/2708606.

13 Plin. *HN.* 35.40 in Pliny the Elder, *Natural History*, trans. H. Rackham, vol. 9 of 10, *Books 33–35*, Loeb Classical Library 394 (Harvard University Press, 1952), 353.

14 Thomas DaCosta Kaufmann, *The Mastery of Nature: Aspects of Art, Science, and Humanism in the Renaissance* (Princeton University Press, 1993), 41–45.

15 Anne Pavord, *The Tulip* (Bloomsbury, 2004), 56–101; and Daniela Bleichmar, *Visible Empire: Botanical Expeditions and Visual Culture in the Hispanic Enlightenment* (University of Chicago Press, 2012), 24–25 passim.

16 Anne Goldgar, *Tulipmania: Money, Honor, and Knowledge in the Dutch Golden Age* (University of Chicago Press, 2008), 110, 200.

17 Carolus Linnaeus, *The "Critica Botanica" of Linnaeus*, trans. Arthur Hort, rev. M. L. Green, with an introduction by Arthur W. Hill (London: Ray Society, 1938), aphorism 259, p. 122.

18 Sam Segal, *Flowers and Nature: Netherlandish Flower Painting of Four Centuries*, trans. Ruth Koenig (Amstelveen: Hijnk International, 1990), 18.

19 Cornelis de Bie, *Het gulden cabinet vande edel vry schilder-const* (Antwerp, 1661), 219.

[20] Charles Baudelaire, "Salon de 1859," in *Curiosités aesthétiques. L'Art romantique et autres œuvres critiques*, ed. Henri Lemaître (Garnier, 1962), 316–20.

[21] Charles de Miramon, "Noble Dogs, Noble Blood: The Invention of the Concept of Race in the Late Middle Ages," in *The Origins of Racism in the West*, ed. Miriam Eliav-Feldon, Benjamin Isaac and Joseph Ziegler (Cambridge University Press, 2009). Pliny consistently uses the Latin word *gens* to refer to these peoples, for which "race" is a misleading translation, because there is no equivalent in either classical or medieval Latin.

[22] Plin. *HN.* 7.2, 5.8 in Pliny the Elder, *Natural History*, trans. H. Rackham, vol. 2 of 10, *Books 3–7*, Loeb Classical Library 352 (Harvard University Press, 1961), 513–27, 248–53; and John Block Friedman, *The Monstrous Races in Medieval Art and Thought* (Harvard University Press, 1981).

[23] Plin. *HN.* 2.80 in Pliny, *Natural History*, 1:320–23.

[24] David Goldenberg, "Racism, Color Symbolism, and Color Prejudice," in Eliav-Feldon, Isaac and Ziegler, *Origins of Racism.*

[25] Augustine of Hippo, *The City of God*, trans. Henry Bettenson (Penguin, 2004), 16.8, p. 662.

[26] C. W. R. D. Moseley, ed. and trans., *The Travels of Sir John Mandeville* (Penguin, 1983), 134; and Susan Conklin Akbari, "The Diversity of Mankind in 'The Book of John Mandeville,'" in *Eastward Bound: Travel and Travellers in the Medieval Mediterranean, 1050–1500*, ed. Rosamund Allen (Manchester University Press, 2004).

[27] Joseph Ziegler, "Physiognomy, Science, and Proto-Racism, 1200–1500," in Eliav-Feldon, Isaac and Ziegler, *Origins of Racism.*

[28] See for example Samuel Stanhope Smith, *An Essay on the Causes of the Variety and Figure in the Human Species* (Philadelphia, 1787).

[29] Valentin Groebner, "*Complexio*/Complexion: Categorizing Individual Nature, 1250–1600," in *The Moral Authority of Nature*, ed. Lorraine Daston and Fernando Vidal (University of Chicago Press, 2004).

[30] Maaike van der Lugt, "Les couleurs de la peau dans les commentaires sur l'*Isagoge* de Johannitius (XIIe–XIIIe siècle)," in *Le corps polychrome: Couleurs et santé. Antiquité, Moyen Âge, Époque moderne*, ed. Franck Collard and Évelyne Samama (L'Harmattan, 2018); see also Peter Biller,

"Proto-Racial Thought in Medieval Science," in Eliav-Feldon, Isaac and Ziegler, *Origins of Racism.*

[31] Herman Pleij, *Colors Demonic and Divine: Shades of Meaning in the Middle Ages and After,* trans. Diane Webb (Columbia University Press, 2004), 50–55.

[32] Robert Bartlett, "Illustrating Ethnicity in the Middle Ages," in Eliav-Feldon, Isaac and Ziegler, *Origins of Racism.*

[33] Giulia Calvi, *The World in Dress: Costume Books across Italy, Europe, and the East* (Cambridge University Press, 2022), 1–29, 49, 75. Calvi estimates that over 200 such books were published in Europe between 1520 and 1610.

[34] Theodor Hampe, *Das Trachtenbuch des Christoph Weiditz von seinen Reisen nach Spanien (1529) und den Niederlanden (1531/32)* (De Gruyter, 1927); and Nicolas de Nicolay, *Discours et histoire veritable des navigations, peregrinations et voyages, faicts en la Turquie* (Antwerp, 1586).

[35] Quoted from a 1585 Bologna description of the arrival of four Japanese noble converts to Christianity in Calvi, *World in Dress,* 70.

[36] Giorgio Riello and Ulinka Rublack, eds., *The Right to Dress: Sumptuary Laws in Global Perspective, c. 1200–1800* (Cambridge University Press, 2019).

[37] Ferrante Imperato, *Dell'historia naturale di Ferrante Imperato Napolitano: Libri XXVIII* (Naples, 1599).

[38] Olaus Worm, *Musaeum Wormianum, seu historia rerum rariorum* (Leiden, 1655).

[39] Nehemiah Grew, *Musaeum Regalis Societatis: Or, A Catalogue & Description of the Natural and Artificial Rarities Belonging to the Royal Society and Preserved at Gresham College* (London, 1681).

[40] Claude du Molinet, *Le Cabinet de la bibliothèque de Sainte Geneviève* (Paris, 1692).

[41] H. J. Witkam, ed., *Catalogues of All the Chiefest Rarities in the Publick Anatomie Hall of the University of Leyden* (Leiden, 1695; repr., Leiden: Witkam, 1980).

[42] Michel de Montaigne, *Journal de voyage en Italie par la Suisse et l'Allemagne en 1580 et 1581,* ed. Maurice Rat (Garnier, 1955), 54.

[43] Francis Bacon, "Gesta Grayorum," in *The Works of Francis Bacon*, eds. James Spedding, Robert Leslie Ellis and Douglas Denon Heath, vol. 8 of 14, *The Letters and the Life: Vol. 1* (London, 1862), 335.

[44] Lorraine Daston and Katharine Park, *Wonders and the Order of Nature, 1150–1750* (Zone Books, 1998), 329–63.

[45] See for example the 2000–2001 Berlin exhibition *Theatrum Naturae et Artis*, Martin-Gropius-Bau, using the collections of the Humboldt-Universität zu Berlin; the 2022 Mantua exhibition *Naturalia et Mirabilia*, Palazzo Ducale, using the collections of the Gonzaga, "Sei conferenze per la *Wunderkammer*," Palazzo Ducale: Complesso museale Mantova, accessed February 7, 2025, https://www.mantovaducale.beniculturali.it/it/news/899-sei-conferenze-per-la-wunderkammer; or the 2022 retrospective of the work of the American artist Rosamund Purcell at the Addison Gallery of American Art, "Rosamund Purcell: Nature Stands Aside," Addison Gallery of American Art, accessed February 6, 2025, https://addison.andover.edu/exhibition/rosamond-purcell-nature-stands-aside/. Numerous museums have used their collections to reconstruct *Wunderkammer*-themed exhibitions.

[46] See for example the blog on Ferrante Imperato on the Biodiversity Heritage Library website: "Ferrante Imperato: Step into His Cabinet of Wonders!," Biodiversity Heritage Library, accessed February 5, 2025, https://blog.biodiversitylibrary.org/2017/03/ferrante-imperato-step-into-his-cabinet-of-wonders.

[47] Mary Beard, *The Roman Triumph* (Harvard University Press, 2007), 107–42; and Steve Mason, "Josephus' Portrait of the Flavian Triumph in Historical and Literary Context," in *Der römische Triumph in Prinzipat und Spätantike*, ed. Fabian Goldbeck and Johannes Wienand (De Gruyter, 2017).

[48] Alexander Bevilacqua, "Race-Making Festivities in Brandenburg-Prussia," *Past & Present* 265, no. 1 (2024): 3–56, https://doi.org/10.1093/pastj/gtae012.

[49] Plin. *HN*. 7.1 in Pliny, *Natural History*, 2:510–13; Augustine, *City of God*, 21.8, p. 981.

[50] Londa Schiebinger and Claudia Swan, eds., *Colonial Botany: Science, Commerce, and Politics in the Early Modern World* (University of Pennsylvania Press, 2005); and Jim Endersby, *Imperial Nature: Joseph Hooker and the Practices of Victorian Science* (University of Chicago Press, 2008).
[51] Carolus Linnaeus, *Hortus Cliffortianus* (Amsterdam, 1737); Carolus Linnaeus, *Musa Cliffortiana*, trans. Stephen Freer with an introduction by Staffan Müller-Wille (Vienna: International Association for Plant Taxonomy, 2007). The frontispiece of the *Hortus Cliffortianus* was drawn and engraved by Jan Wandelaar, who also wrote the accompanying verses.

Chapter Two

[1] Charles Darwin, *On the Origin of Species*, with an introduction by Ernst Mayr (London, 1859; facsimile ed., Harvard University Press, 1964), 490.
[2] "It is through wonder that men now begin and originally began to philosophize": Arist. *Metaph.* 1.2.982b11–14. The translation is quoted from Aristotle, *Metaphysics*, trans. Hugh Tredennick, vol. 1 of 2, *Books 1–9*, Loeb Classical Library 271 (Harvard University Press, 1989), 13.
[3] [Alexandre Deleyre], "Épingle," in *Encyclopédie, ou Dictionnaire raisonné des arts, des sciences et des métiers*, eds. Denis Diderot and Jean-Baptiste le Rond d'Alembert, vol. 5 of 17 (Paris, 1755); see also [Jean-Rodolphe Perronet], "Épinglier," in *Recueil de planches, sur les sciences, les arts libéraux et les arts méchaniques, avec leur explication*, eds. Denis Diderot and Jean-Baptiste le Rond d'Alembert, vol. 4 of 11 (Paris, 1765).
[4] Adam Smith, *The Wealth of Nations*, ed. Edward Cannan (University of Chicago Press, 1976), 11–14. On Darwin's debt to British economic thought, see Silvan S. Schweber, "The Wider British Context in Darwin's Theorizing," in *The Darwinian Heritage*, ed. David Kohn (Princeton University Press, 1985).
[5] Gunnar Broberg, *The Man Who Organized Nature: The Life of Linnaeus* (Princeton University Press, 2023), 279.
[6] Henri Milne-Edwards, *Introduction à la zoologie générale, ou Considérations sur les tendances de la nature* (Paris, 1851), 7, 9, 35.

[7] Darwin, *Origin of Species*, 115–16.

[8] Carolus Linnaeus [Isaac Biberg], *Specimen academicum de oeconomia naturae* (Uppsala, 1749), quoted in Trevor Pearce, "'A Great Complication of Circumstances': Darwin and the Economy of Nature," *Journal of the History of Biology* 43, no. 3 (2010): 497, https://doi.org/10.1007/s10739-009-9205-0. Although Biberg defended the dissertation, it was written by Linnaeus, as was the custom of the time at many European universities, see William Clark, *Academic Charisma and the Origins of the Research University* (University of Chicago Press, 2006), 204–11.

[9] Christian Daniel Wilcke, "On the Police of Nature," in *Select Dissertations from the Amoenitates Academicae*, trans. F. J. Brand (London, 1781), 1:132–35, 158, 164.

[10] Charles Lyell, *Principles of Geology*, vol. 2 of 3 (London, 1832; facsimile ed., University of Chicago Press, 1991), 159–73, 183; and David Sepkoski, *Catastrophic Thinking: Extinction and the Value of Diversity from Darwin to the Anthropocene* (University of Chicago Press, 2020), 36–46.

[11] Darwin, *Origin of Species*, 67. On Darwin's modification of earlier ideas of the economy of nature and especially the importance of "stations," see Pearce, "'Great Complication.'"

[12] Quoted in Pearce, "'Great Complication,'" 507.

[13] Darwin, *Origin of Species*, 129–30.

[14] Darwin, *Origin of Species*, 83. Alfred Russell Wallace recommended, apropos of this passage and others, that Darwin adopt Herbert Spencer's phrase "survival of the fittest" in place of "natural selection," in order to dispel any impression of an "*intelligent chooser*": Alfred Russell Wallace to Charles Darwin, Hurstpierpoint, Sussex, July 2, 1866, in *Darwin Correspondence Project*, "Letter no. 5140," accessed September 8, 2025, https://www.darwinproject.ac.uk/letter/?docId=letters/DCP-LETT-5140.xml.

[15] Charles Darwin, *The Various Contrivances by Which Orchids Are Fertilised by Insects*, 2nd rev. ed. (London, 1877), 43, 179.

[16] Charles Darwin to Joseph Dalton Hooker, Down, Bromley, formerly Kent, June 5, 1860, in *Darwin Correspondence Project*, "Letter no. 2821," accessed February 19, 2025, https://www.darwinproject.ac.uk/letter/?docId=letters/DCP-LETT-2821.xml.

[17] Darwin, *Various Contrivances*, 20–24, 31.
[18] Darwin, *Various Contrivances*, 152–53.
[19] Darwin, *Various Contrivances*, 286.
[20] Darwin designates this group as a tribe, but botanists now consider it a genus (called *Ophrys*) of the *Orchidiae.*
[21] Darwin, *Various Contrivances*, 264.
[22] Charles Darwin to Asa Gray, Down, Bromley, formerly Kent, April 3, 1860, in *Darwin Correspondence Project*, "Letter no. 2743," accessed February 20, 2025, https://www.darwinproject.ac.uk/letter/?docId=letters/DCP-LETT-2743.xml.
[23] Thierry Hocquet and Michael Levandowsky, "Utility vs. Beauty: Darwin, Wallace and the Subsequent History of the Debate on Sexual Selection," in *Current Perspectives on Sexual Selection: What's Left after Darwin?*, ed. Thierry Hocquet (Springer, 2015).
[24] Charles Darwin, *The Descent of Man, and Selection in Relation to Sex*, with an introduction by John Tyler Bonner and Robert M. May (London, 1871; repr., Princeton University Press, 1981), 2:39.
[25] Darwin, *Descent of Man*, 1:63–4.
[26] On the history of the debate, see Helena Cronin, *The Ant and the Peacock: Altruism and Sexual Selection from Darwin to Today* (Cambridge University Press, 1991); Erika Lorraine Milam, *Looking for a Few Good Males: Female Choice in Evolutionary Biology* (Johns Hopkins University Press, 2010); and Hocquet and Levandowsky, "Utility vs. Beauty."
[27] Amotz Zahavi and Avishag Zahavi, *The Handicap Principle: A Missing Piece of Darwin's Puzzle* (Oxford University Press, 1997); and Raghavendra Gadagkar, "Is the Peacock Merely Beautiful or Also Honest?," *Current Science* 85, no. 7 (2003): 1012–20, https://www.jstor.org/stable/24108784.
[28] Richard O. Prum, "Genetic Evolution by Mate Choice: Darwin's 'Really' Dangerous Idea," *Philosophical Transactions of the Royal Society: Biological Sciences* 367, no. 1600 (2012): 2253–65, https://doi.org/10.1098/rstb.2011.0285.
[29] Carolus Linnaeus, "Curiositas naturalis," in *L'Équilibre de la nature*, ed. Camille Limoges, trans. Bernard Jasmin (Paris: Vrin, 1972), 136–37.
[30] Darwin, *Descent of Man*, 2:353–54.

Chapter Three

[1] Hdt. 2.35 in Herodotus, *The History*, trans. David Grene (University of Chicago Press, 1987), 145.

[2] Charles Louis de Secondat, Baron de La Brède et de Montesquieu, *De l'Esprit des lois* (Paris, 1849), bk. XIV, chaps. 1–10, pp. 187–195.

[3] Marie Jean Antoine Nicolas Caritat, Marquis de Condorcet, "Observations de Condorcet sur le vingt-neuvième livre de *l'Esprit des lois*," in *Œuvres de Condorcet*, eds. A. Condorcet-O'Connor and François Arago, vol. 1 of 12 (Paris, 1847), 378.

[4] On the actual implementation of these programs, see Frank Dobbin, *Inventing Equal Opportunity* (Princeton University Press, 2009).

[5] This account of US and European Union developments draws heavily on the cogent overview by Steven Vertovec, "'Diversity' and the Social Imaginary," *European Journal of Sociology* 53, no. 3 (2012): 287–312, https://doi.org/10.1017/S000397561200015X.

[6] Quoted in David B. Oppenheimer, "Archibald Cox and the Diversity Justification for Affirmative Action," *Virginia Journal of Social Policy and Law* 25, no. 2 (2018): 158–203, https://dx.doi.org/10.2139/ssrn.2913310. Oppenheimer has traced the arguments and examples used by Justice Powell to an *amicus curiae* brief written by Harvard legal scholar Archibald Cox for the earlier DeFunis case, dismissed as moot.

[7] Nicolas Lemann, "Can Affirmative Action Survive?" *The New Yorker*, July 26, 2021, https://www.newyorker.com/magazine/2021/08/02/can-affirmative-action-survive; and Nicolas Langlitz and Clemente de Althaus, "The Moral Economy of Diversity: How the Epistemic Value of Diversity Transforms Late Modern Knowledge Cultures," *History of the Human Sciences* 37, no. 1 (2023): 1–25, https://doi.org/10.1177/09526951231166533.

[8] Lemann, "Can Affirmative Action Survive?," quotes Columbia University law professor Jamal Greene's view that the diversity justification permits "schools—with the Court's blessing—to pursue racial justice in the shadows."

[9] Richard A. Posner, "The DeFunis Case and the Constitutionality of Preferential Treatment of Racial Minorities," *The Supreme Court Review* 1974 (1974): 1–32, https://doi.org/10.1086/scr.1974.3108703.

[10] *Students for Fair Admissions, Inc. v. President and Fellows of Harvard College*, 600 US 181 (2023). The case was decided on June 29, 2023.
[11] The fissures within this consensus emerged when it came to defining what kind of diversity counted: race? Gender? Political affiliation? Neurological constitution? See Langlitz and de Althaus, "Moral Economy of Diversity."
[12] Quoted in Valerie Møller, Helga Dickow and Mari Harris, "South Africa's 'Rainbow People.' National Pride and Happiness," *Social Indicators Research* 47, no. 3 (1999): 252, https://doi.org/10.1023/A:1006945108139.
[13] Nelson Mandela, "Let Freedom Reign: Pretoria, 10 May 1994," in *Let Freedom Reign: The Words of Nelson Mandela*, ed. Henry Russell (Northampton, MA: Interlink Books, 2010), 96.
[14] Fredrick Gordon Brownell, "Convergence and Unification: The National Flag of South Africa (1994) in Historical Perspective" (PhD diss., University of Pretoria, 2015), 160, 184, 199, https://hdl.handle.net/2263/50847. Brownell was the South African State Herald and was himself responsible for the final design of the flag.
[15] Lemann, "Can Affirmative Action Survive?"
[16] Alain Desrosières, *The Politics of Large Numbers*, trans. Camille Naish (Harvard University Press, 1998), 236–78.
[17] Mandela, "Let Freedom Reign," 95.
[18] Steven Vertovec, "Introduction: Formulating Diversity Studies," in *Routledge International Handbook of Diversity Studies*, ed. Steven Vertovec (Routledge, 2015), 2.
[19] John Wrench, "Diversity Management," in Vertovec, *Handbook of Diversity Studies*, 258.
[20] Anne Fausto-Sterling, *Myths of Gender: Biological Theories about Women and Men* (Basic Books, 1985), 90–122.
[21] John Carson, *The Measure of Merit: Talents, Intelligence, and Inequality in the French and American Republics, 1750–1940* (Princeton University Press, 2007), 75–109.
[22] Ronald Bayer, "Politics, Science, and the Problem of Psychiatric Nomenclature: A Case Study of the American Psychiatric Association Referendum on Homosexuality," in *Scientific Controversies: Case Studies in the*

Resolution and Closure of Disputes in Science and Technology, eds. H. Tristram Engelhardt, Jr., and Arthur L. Caplan (Cambridge University Press, 2010).

[23] Helen Longino, *Science as Social Knowledge: Values and Objectivity in Scientific Inquiry* (Princeton University Press, 1990), 76–79.

[24] Kerri Smith, "Women's Health Research Lacks Funding: These Charts Show How," *Nature*, May 3, 2023, https://www.nature.com/immersive/d41586-023-01475-2/index.html.

[25] Sandra Harding, *Sciences from Below: Feminisms, Postcolonialities, and Modernities* (Duke University Press, 2008); and Sandra Harding, *Objectivity and Diversity: Another Logic of Scientific Research* (University of Chicago Press, 2015).

[26] Michael Fischer, "Diversity Management and the Business Case," in *Equal Opportunities and Ethnic Inequality in European Labour Markets*, eds. Karen Kraal, Judith Roosblad and John Wrench (University of Amsterdam Press, 2009).

[27] Cara Tannenbaum et al. "Sex and Gender Analysis Improves Science and Engineering," *Nature* 575 (2019): 137–46, https://doi.org/10.1038/s41586-019-1657-6.

[28] For an attempt to untangle some of these factors, see Bas Hofstra et al., "The Diversity-Innovation Paradox in Science," *Proceedings of the National Academy of Sciences (PNAS)* 117, no. 17 (2020): 9284–91, https://doi.org/10.1073/pnas.1915378117.

[29] Alana Lentin and Gavan Titley, "More Benetton than Barricades? The Politics of Diversity in Europe," in *The Politics of Diversity in Europe*, eds. Alana Lentin and Gavan Titley (Strasbourg: Council of Europe Publishing, 2008), 9–28.

[30] Jason Brennan, "Diversity for Justice vs. Diversity for Performance," *Journal of Business Ethics* 187 (2023): 433–47, https://doi.org/10.1007/s10551-022-05278-9.

[31] Fernando Vidal and Nélia Dias, "Introduction: The Endangerment Sensibility," in *Endangerment, Biodiversity and Culture*, eds. Fernando Vidal and Nélia Dias (Routledge, 2016).

Bibliography

Addison Gallery of American Art. "Rosamund Purcell: Nature Stands Aside." Accessed February 6, 2025. https://addison.andover.edu/exhibition/rosamond-purcell-nature-stands-aside/.

Akbari, Susan Conklin. "The Diversity of Mankind in 'The Book of John Mandeville.'" In *Eastward Bound: Travel and Travellers in the Medieval Mediterranean 1050–1500*, edited by Rosamund Allen. Manchester University Press, 2004.

Aristotle. *Metaphysics.* Translated by Hugh Tredennick. Vol. 1 of 2, *Books 1–9.* Loeb Classical Library 271. Harvard University Press, 1989.

Augustine of Hippo. *The City of God.* Translated by Henry Bettenson. Penguin, 2004.

Bacon, Francis. "Gesta Grayorum." In *The Works of Francis Bacon*, edited by James Spedding, Robert Leslie Ellis and Douglas Denon Heath. Vol. 8 of 14, *The Letters and the Life: Vol. 1.* London, 1862.

Bartholomeus Anglicus. *De genuinis rerum coelestium, terrarum et inferarum proprietatibus libri XVIII.* Frankfurt, 1601.

Bartlett, Robert. "Illustrating Ethnicity in the Middle Ages." In Eliav-Feldon, Isaac and Ziegler, *Origins of Racism.*

Baudelaire, Charles. "Salon de 1859." In *Curiosités aesthétiques. L'Art romantique et autres œuvres critiques*, edited by Henri Lemaître. Garnier, 1962.

Bayer, Ronald. "Politics, Science, and the Problem of Psychiatric Nomenclature: A Case Study of the American Psychiatric Association

Referendum on Homosexuality." In *Scientific Controversies: Case Studies in the Resolution and Closure of Disputes in Science and Technology*, edited by H. Tristram Engelhardt, Jr., and Arthur L. Caplan. Cambridge University Press, 2010.

Beard, Mary. *The Roman Triumph*. Harvard University Press, 2007.

Bevilacqua, Alexander. "Race-Making Festivities in Brandenburg-Prussia." *Past & Present* 265, no. 1 (2024): 3–56. https://doi.org/10.1093/pastj/gtae012.

Bie, Cornelis de. *Het gulden cabinet vande edel vry schilder-const*. Antwerp, 1661.

Biller, Peter. "Proto-Racial Thought in Medieval Science." In Eliav-Feldon, Isaac and Ziegler, *Origins of Racism*.

Biodiversity Heritage Library. "Ferrante Imperato: Step into His Cabinet of Wonders!" Accessed February 5, 2025. https://blog.biodiversitylibrary.org/2017/03/ferrante-imperato-step-into-his-cabinet-of-wonders.

Bleichmar, Daniela. *Visible Empire: Botanical Expeditions and Visual Culture in the Hispanic Enlightenment*. University of Chicago Press, 2012.

Boodt, Anselm de. *Gemmarum et lapidum historia*. Leiden, 1647.

Boyle, Robert. *An Essay About the Origine and Virtues of Gems*. London, 1672.

Brennan, Jason. "Diversity for Justice vs. Diversity for Performance." *Journal of Business Ethics* 187 (2023): 433–47. https://doi.org/10.1007/s10551-022-05278-9.

Broberg, Gunnar. *The Man Who Organized Nature: The Life of Linnaeus*. Princeton University Press, 2023.

Brownell, Fredrick Gordon. "Convergence and Unification: The National Flag of South Africa (1994) in Historical Perspective." PhD diss., University of Pretoria, 2015. https://hdl.handle.net/2263/50847.

Calvi, Giulia. *The World in Dress: Costume Books across Italy, Europe, and the East*. Cambridge University Press, 2022.

Carson, John. *The Measure of Merit: Talents, Intelligence, and Inequality in the French and American Republics, 1750–1940*. Princeton University Press, 2007.

Clark, William. *Academic Charisma and the Origins of the Research University* University of Chicago Press, 2006.

Close, A. J. "Commonplace Theories of Art and Nature in Classical Antiquity and in the Renaissance." *Journal of the History of Ideas* 30, no. 4 (1969): 467–86. https://doi.org/10.2307/2708606.

Condorcet, Marie Jean Antoine Nicolas Caritat, Marquis de. "Observations de Condorcet sur le vingt-neuvième livre de *l'Esprit des lois*." In *Œuvres de Condorcet*. Edited by A. Condorcet-O'Connor and François Arago. Vol. 1 of 12. Paris, 1847.

Cronin, Helena. *The Ant and the Peacock: Altruism and Sexual Selection from Darwin to Today*. Cambridge University Press, 1991.

Darwin, Charles. Charles Darwin to Asa Gray, Down, Bromley, formerly Kent, April 3, 1860. In *Darwin Correspondence Project*. "Letter no. 2743." Accessed February 20, 2025. https://www.darwinproject.ac.uk/letter/?docId=letters/DCP-LETT-2743.xml.

Darwin, Charles. Charles Darwin to Joseph Dalton Hooker, Down, Bromley, formerly Kent, June 5, 1860. In *Darwin Correspondence Project*. "Letter no. 2821." Accessed February 19, 2025. https://www.darwinproject.ac.uk/letter/?docId=letters/DCP-LETT-2821.xml.

Darwin, Charles. *The Descent of Man, and Selection in Relation to Sex*. 2 vols. London, 1871. Reprint, with an introduction by John Tyler Bonner and Robert M. May. Princeton University Press, 1981.

Darwin, Charles. *On the Origin of Species*. London, 1859. Facsimile of the first edition, with an introduction by Ernst Mayr. Harvard University Press, 1964.

Darwin, Charles. *The Various Contrivances by Which Orchids Are Fertilised by Insects*. 2nd rev. ed. London, 1877.

Darwin, Francis. *The Life and Letters of Charles Darwin*. 3rd ed. Vol. 2. London, 1887.

Daston, Lorraine, and Katharine Park. *Wonders and the Order of Nature, 1150–1750*. Zone Books, 1998.

[Deleyre, Alexandre]. "Épingle." In *Encyclopédie, ou Dictionnaire raisonné des arts, des sciences et des métiers*, edited by Denis Diderot and Jean-Baptiste le Rond d'Alembert. Vol. 5 of 17. Paris, 1755.

Desrosières, Alain. *The Politics of Large Numbers*. Translated by Camille Naish. Harvard University Press, 1998.

Dobbin, Frank. *Inventing Equal Opportunity*. Princeton University Press, 2009.

Eliav-Feldon, Miriam, Benjamin Isaac and Joseph Ziegler, eds. *The Origins of Racism in the West*. Cambridge University Press, 2009.

Endersby, Jim. *Imperial Nature: Joseph Hooker and the Practices of Victorian Science*. University of Chicago Press, 2008.

Fausto-Sterling, Anne. *Myths of Gender: Biological Theories about Women and Men*. Basic Books, 1985.

Fischer, Michael. "Diversity Management and the Business Case." In *Equal Opportunities and Ethnic Inequality in European Labour Markets*, edited by Karen Kraal, Judith Roosblad and John Wrench. University of Amsterdam Press, 2009.

Friedman, John Block. *The Monstrous Races in Medieval Art and Thought*. Harvard University Press, 1981.

Goldenberg, David. "Racism, Color Symbolism, and Color Prejudice." In Eliav-Feldon, Isaac and Ziegler, *Origins of Racism*.

Goldgar, Anne. *Tulipmania: Money, Honor, and Knowledge in the Dutch Golden Age*. University of Chicago Press, 2008.

Grew, Nehemiah. *Musaeum Regalis Societatis: Or, A Catalogue & Description of the Natural and Artificial Rarities Belonging to the Royal Society and Preserved at Gresham College*. London, 1681.

Groebner, Valentin. "*Complexio*/Complexion: Categorizing Individual Nature, 1250–1600." In *The Moral Authority of Nature*, edited by Lorraine Daston and Fernando Vidal. University of Chicago Press, 2004.

Hampe, Theodor. *Das Trachtenbuch des Christoph Weiditz von seinen Reisen nach Spanien (1529) und den Niederlanden (1531/32)*. De Gruyter, 1927.

Harding, Sandra. *Objectivity and Diversity: Another Logic of Scientific Research*. University of Chicago Press, 2015.

Harding, Sandra. *Sciences from Below: Feminisms, Postcolonialities, and Modernities*. Duke University Press, 2008.

Heinich, Nathalie. "Framing the Bull Fight: Aesthetics versus Ethics." *British Journal of Aesthetics* 33, no. 1 (1993): 52–58. https://doi.org/10.1093/bjaesthetics/33.1.52.

Herodotus. *The History*. Translated by David Grene. University of Chicago Press, 1987.

Hocquet, Thierry, and Michael Levandowsky. "Utility vs. Beauty: Darwin, Wallace and the Subsequent History of the Debate on Sexual Selection." In *Current Perspectives on Sexual Selection: What's Left after Darwin?*, edited by Thierry Hocquet. Springer, 2015.

Hofstra, Bas, Vivek. V. Kulkarni, Sebastian Munoz-Najar Galvez, Bryan He, Dan Jurafsky and Daniel McFarland. "The Diversity-Innovation Paradox in Science." *Proceedings of the National Academy of Sciences (PNAS)* 117, no. 17 (2020): 9284–92. https://doi.org/10.1073/pnas.1915378117.

Humphreys, Sally. "Law, Custom and Culture in Herodotus." *Arethusa* 20, no. 1/2 (1987): 211–20. http://www.jstor.org/stable/44578858.

Imperato, Ferrante. *Dell'historia naturale di Ferrante Imperato Napolitano: Libri XXVIII*. Naples, 1599.

Kant, Immanuel. *Kritik der Urteilskraft*. Edited by Wilhelm Weischedel. Suhrkamp, 1974.

Kaufmann, Thomas DaCosta. *The Mastery of Nature: Aspects of Art, Science, and Humanism in the Renaissance*. Princeton University Press, 1993.

Langlitz, Nicolas, and Clemente de Althaus. "The Moral Economy of Diversity: How the Epistemic Value of Diversity Transforms Late Modern Knowledge Cultures." *History of the Human Sciences* 37, no. 1 (2023): 1–25. https://doi.org/10.1177/09526951231166533.

Lemann, Nicolas. "Can Affirmative Action Survive?" *The New Yorker*, July 26, 2021. https://www.newyorker.com/magazine/2021/08/02/can-affirmative-action-survive.

Lentin, Alana, and Gavan Titley. "More Benetton than Barricades? The Politics of Diversity in Europe." In *The Politics of Diversity in Europe*, edited by Alana Lentin and Gavan Titley. Strasbourg: Council of Europe Publishing, 2008.

Linnaeus, Carolus. *The "Critica Botanica" of Linnaeus*. Translated by Arthur Hort. Revised by M. L. Green, with an introduction by Arthur W. Hill. London: Ray Society, 1938.

Linnaeus, Carolus. "Curiositas naturalis." In *L'Équilibre de la nature*. Edited by Camille Limoges. Translated by Bernard Jasmin. Paris: Vrin, 1972.

Linnaeus, Carolus. *Hortus Cliffortianus*. Amsterdam, 1737.

Linnaeus, Carolus. *Musa Cliffortiana*. Translated by Stephen Freer, with an introduction by Staffan Müller-Wille. Vienna: International Association for Plant Taxonomy, 2007.

Linnaeus, Carolus, [and Isaac Biberg]. *Specimen academicum de oeconomia naturae*. Uppsala, 1749.

Longino, Helen. *Science as Social Knowledge: Values and Objectivity in Scientific Inquiry*. Princeton University Press, 1990.

Lugt, Maaike van der. "Les couleurs de la peau dans les commentaires sur l'*Isagoge* de Johannitius (XIIe–XIIIe siècle)." In *Le corps polychrome: Couleurs et santé. Antiquité, Moyen Âge, Époque moderne*, edited by Franck Collard and Évelyne Samama. L'Harmattan, 2018.

Lyell, Charles. *Principles of Geology*. Vol. 2 of 3. London, 1832. Facsimile edition. University of Chicago Press, 1991.

Mandela, Nelson. "Let Freedom Reign: Pretoria, 10 May 1994." In *Let Freedom Reign: The Words of Nelson Mandela*, edited by Henry Russell. Northampton, MA: Interlink Books, 2010.

Mason, Steve. "Josephus' Portrait of the Flavian Triumph in Historical and Literary Context." In *Der römische Triumph in Prinzipat und Spätantike*, edited by Fabian Goldbeck and Johannes Wienand. De Gruyter, 2017.

Milam, Erika Lorraine. *Looking for a Few Good Males: Female Choice in Evolutionary Biology*. Johns Hopkins University Press, 2010.

Milne-Edwards, Henri. *Introduction à la zoologie générale, ou Considérations sur les tendances de la nature* Paris, 1851.

Miramon, Charles de. "Noble Dogs, Noble Blood: The Invention of the Concept of Race in the Late Middle Ages." In Eliav-Feldon, Isaac and Ziegler, *Origins of Racism*.

Molinet, Claude du. *Le Cabinet de la bibliothèque de Sainte Geneviève* Paris, 1692.

Møller, Valerie, Helga Dickow and Mari Harris. "South Africa's 'Rainbow People.' National Pride and Happiness." *Social Indicators Research* 47, no. 3 (1999): 245–80. https://doi.org/10.1023/A:1006945108139.

Montaigne, Michel de. *Journal de voyage en Italie par la Suisse et l'Allemagne en 1580 et 1581.* Edited by Maurice Rat. Garnier, 1955.

Montesquieu, Charles Louis de Secondat, Baron de La Brède et de. *De l'Esprit des lois.* Paris, 1849.

Moseley, C. W. R. D. ed. and trans. *The Travels of Sir John Mandeville.* Penguin, 1983.

Nicolay, Nicolas de. *Discours et histoire veritable des navigations, peregrinations et voyages, faicts en la Turquie.* Antwerp, 1586.

Oppenheimer, David B. "Archibald Cox and the Diversity Justification for Affirmative Action." *Virginia Journal of Social Policy and Law* 25, no. 2 (2018): 158–203. https://dx.doi.org/10.2139/ssrn.2913310.

Palazzo Ducale: Complesso museale Mantova. "Sei conferenze per la *Wunderkammer.*" Accessed February 7, 2025. https://www.mantovaducale.beniculturali.it/it/news/899-sei-conferenze-per-la-wunderkammer.

Pavord, Anne. *The Tulip.* Bloomsbury, 2004.

Pearce, Trevor. "'A Great Complication of Circumstances': Darwin and the Economy of Nature." *Journal of the History of Biology* 43, no. 3 (2010): 493–528. https://doi.org/10.1007/s10739-009-9205-0.

[Perronet, Jean-Rodolphe]. "Épinglier." In *Recueil de planches, sur les sciences, les arts libéraux et les arts méchaniques, avec leur explication*, edited by Denis Diderot and Jean-Baptiste le Rond d'Alembert, Vol. 4 of 11. Paris, 1765.

Pleij, Herman. *Colors Demonic and Divine: Shades of Meaning in the Middle Ages and After.* Translated by Diane Webb. Columbia University Press, 2004.

Pliny the Elder. *Natural History.* Rev. ed. Translated by H. Rackham. Vol. 1 of 10, *Books 1–2.* Loeb Classical Library 330. Harvard University Press, 1949.

Pliny the Elder. *Natural History.* Translated by H. Rackham. Vol. 2 of 10, *Books 3–7.* Loeb Classical Library 352. Harvard University Press, 1961.

Pliny the Elder. *Natural History.* Translated by W. H. S. Jones. Vol. 6 of 10, *Books 20–23.* Loeb Classical Library 392. Harvard University Press, 1951.

Pliny the Elder. *Natural History.* Translated by H. Rackham. Vol. 9 of 10, *Books 33–35.* Loeb Classical Library 394. Harvard University Press, 1952.

Pliny the Elder. *Natural History.* Translated by D. E. Eichholz. Vol. 10 of 10, *Books 36–37.* Loeb Classical Library 419. Harvard University Press, 1962.

Posner, Richard A. "The DeFunis Case and the Constitutionality of Preferential Treatment of Racial Minorities." *The Supreme Court Review* 1974 (1974): 1–32. https://doi.org/10.1086/scr.1974.3108703.

Prum, Richard O. "Genetic Evolution by Mate Choice: Darwin's 'Really' Dangerous Idea." *Philosophical Transactions of the Royal Society: Biological Sciences* 367, no. 1600 (2012): 2253–65, https://doi.org/10.1098/rstb.2011.0285.

Raghavendra Gadagkar. "Is the Peacock Merely Beautiful or Also Honest?" *Current Science* 85, no. 7 (2003): 1012–1020. https://www.jstor.org/stable/24108784.

Riello, Giorgio, and Ulinka Rublack, eds. *The Right to Dress: Sumptuary Laws in Global Perspective, c. 1200–1800.* Cambridge University Press, 2019.

Schiebinger, Londa, and Claudia Swan, eds. *Colonial Botany: Science, Commerce, and Politics in the Early Modern World.* University of Pennsylvania Press, 2005.

Schweber, Silvan S. "The Wider British Context in Darwin's Theorizing." In *The Darwinian Heritage*, edited by David Kohn. Princeton University Press, 1985.

Segal, Sam. *Flowers and Nature: Netherlandish Flower Painting of Four Centuries.* Translated by Ruth Koenig. Amstelveen: Hijnk International, 1990.

Sepkoski, David. *Catastrophic Thinking: Extinction and the Value of Diversity from Darwin to the Anthropocene.* University of Chicago Press, 2020.

Smith, Adam. *The Wealth of Nations.* Edited by Edward Cannan. University of Chicago Press, 1976.

Smith, Kerri. "Women' Health Research Lacks Funding: These Charts Show How." *Nature*, May 3, 2023. https://www.nature.com/immersive/d41586-023-01475-2/index.html.

Smith, Samuel Stanhope. *An Essay on the Causes of the Variety and Figure in the Human Species.* Philadelphia, 1787.

Students for Fair Admissions, Inc. v. President and Fellows of Harvard College, 600 US 181 (2023).

Tannenbaum, Cara, Robert P. Ellis, Friederike Eyssel, James Zou and Londa Schiebinger. "Sex and Gender Analysis Improves Science and Engineering." *Nature* 575 (2019): 137–46. https://doi.org/10.1038/s41586-019-1657-6.

Vertovec, Steven. "'Diversity' and the Social Imaginary." *European Journal of Sociology* 53, no. 3 (2012): 287–312. https://doi.org/10.1017/S000397561200015X.

Vertovec, Steven. "Introduction: Formulating Diversity Studies." In Vertovec, *Handbook of Diversity Studies.*

Vertovec, Steven, ed. *Routledge International Handbook of Diversity Studies*. Routledge, 2015.

Vidal, Fernando, and Nélia Dias. "Introduction: The Endangerment Sensibility." In *Endangerment, Biodiversity and Culture*, edited by Fernando Vidal and Nélia Dias. Routledge, 2016.

Wallace, Alfred Russell. Alfred Russell Wallace to Charles Darwin, Hurstpierpoint, Sussex, July 2, 1866. In *Darwin Correspondence*

Project. "Letter no. 5140." Accessed September 8, 2025. https://www.darwinproject.ac.uk/letter/?docId=letters/DCP-LETT-5140.xml.

Wilcke, Christian Daniel. "On the Police of Nature." In *Select Dissertations from the Amoenitates Academicae.* Translated by F. J. Brand. Vol. 1. London, 1781.

Witkam, H. J., ed. *Catalogues of All the Chiefest Rarities in the Publick Anatomie Hall of the University of Leyden.* Leiden, 1695. Reprint, Leiden: Witkam, 1980.

Worm, Ole. *Musaeum Wormianum, seu historia rerum rariorum.* Leiden, 1655.

Wrench, John. "Diversity Management." In Vertovec, *Handbook of Diversity Studies.*

Zahavi, Amotz, and Avishag Zahavi. *The Handicap Principle: A Missing Piece of Darwin's Puzzle.* Oxford University Press, 1997.

Ziegler, Joseph. "Physiognomy, Science, and Protoracism, 1200–1500." In Eliav-Feldon, Isaac and Ziegler, *Origins of Racism.*

Index

Aesthetics (see also Beauty), 12
Affirmative Action, 92–93
Alembert, Jean-Baptiste le Rond d', 54
Alexander the Great, 21, 39
Augustine of Hippo, 24–25, 41
Aristotle, 16, 48, 77

Babbage, Charles, 55
Bacon, Francis, 36
Bakke, Allen, 94, 96
Beauty, of flowers, 14–19; of gemstones, 15–16; as opposed to utility, 15–16, 51, 73–76; linked to utility, 57, 60; of orchids, 72–73; of bird feathers, 73–76; Darwin on standards of, 79–80
Bie, Cornelis de, 19
Biodiversity, 20, 38, Darwin on 47–53; Linnaeus on, 57, 61; source of wonder, 77–80
Boyle, Robert, 16

Charlemagne, 39
Charles V (Holy Roman Emperor), 21, 28, 30, 40–41
Civil Rights movement, 91
Clifford, George, 19, 44
Conant, James Bryant, 95
Condorcet, Marie Jean Antoine Nicolas de Caritat, marquis de, 87–90, 112–113
Cortes, Hernán, 40

Darwin, Charles, 16, on biodiversity, 47–53; on extinction, 52–53, 66–

67; on orchids, 68–73; on nature's contrivances, 69–71, 77; on beauty of organisms, 73–76; on standards of beauty, 79–80
Davis, Natalie Zemon, 6
Desrais, Claude-Louis, 56
Diderot, Denis, 53, 54
Diversity (see also Beauty, Biodiversity, Efficiency, Justice, Values), as a moral intuition, 10, 108; as aesthetic value, 13–45; of humans, 21–33; of organisms, 47–53; as economic value, 47–80; as a political value, 81–114; Diversity-Equity-Inclusion (DEI), 83; frequency of word usage, 83–84; difficulties of definition, 86, 90, 107; as opposed to universalism, 82, 87–90; European Union directives concerning, 93; legal decisions concerning, 95–97; role of South Africa in popularizing, 97–99; and identity, 100, 103, 106–107, 113–114; in science, 103–106
Division of labor, 52, in pin factory, 53–55, 113; in society, 55–57; in physiology, 55–60; among organisms, 64–68
Douglass, Frederick, 81–82
Dress, as marker of ethnicity, 28–32; as marker of social status, 30–32
Dürer, Albrecht, 18, 35
Durkheim, Émile, 55
Dutch East India Company, 44

Efficiency (see also Division of Labor), of organisms, 51, 57–60; of economies, 53–57; of businesses, 102–103
Empire, 38–44
Engels, Friedrich, 82
Enlightenment, 82; conflicting values of, 87–90, 112–113
Equality, as contrasted to diversity, 9–10, 81–87; Equal Employment Opportunity, 92–93
Extinction, 52–53, 62–66

Ferdinand II of Tyrol, 35, 38
Flowers (see also Orchids), as emblem of diversity 13–15, 20, 45, 101; in painting, 16–20; as example of pure aesthetic value, 17; in gardens, 18–19, 42–44

Foucault, Michel, 9
Francken, Frans the Younger, 41
Franz Joseph I (emperor of Austria, king of Hungary), 37

Galen, 26
Gemstones, 15–16
Glycera, 17
Google N-Grams, 83–85
Grotius, Hugo, 89
Gray, Asa, 73

Haeckel, Ernst, 65
Harvard University, 94–99
Heem, Jan Davidsz de, 19
Henri II, king of France, 28
Herodotus, 8, 21, 88
Hoefnagel, Joris, 34
Hooker, Joseph Dalton, 70
Hume, David, 37

Imperato, Ferrante, 33, 34
Isidore of Seville, 21

Julius Caesar, 21, 39
Justice, as equality, 91–92; reparative, 96, 100; as diversity, 99–101

Kahn, Fritz, 59
Kant, Immanuel, 3, 12
Kubla Khan (emperor Shizu of Yuan), 27

Linnaeus, Carolus von, 19, 37, 43, 44, 52; on biodiversity, 57; on economy of nature, 60–67
Lyell, Charles, 52; on extinction, 62–64

Malthus, Thomas, 64
Mandela, Nelson, 97–98, 101
Marx, Karl, 82
Mill, John Stuart, 95
Milne-Edwards, Henri, 57–58
Mondrian, Piet, 20
Montaigne, Michel de, 35
Montesquieu, Charles Louis de Secondat, baron de, 87–90, 112–113
Museums, 36–38

Natural law, 89–90
Natural selection, 64–68
Natural theology, 60–63, 73, 77–78
Nicolay, Nicolas de, 28, 29, 31, 39
Nietzsche, Friedrich, 8

Orchids, 68–73
Origen, 27

Pausias, 17, 18
Pliny the Elder, 38, 73; on flowers and gemstones, 13–16, 41–42, 47, 51, 67, 101; on nature at play, 14, 68, 80; on human diversity 21–25; early modern reception of, 33–34
Polo, Marco, 21, 27, 32
Powell, Lewis, 94, 99
Pufendorf, Samuel, 89

Races, Pliny's exotic, 22–24; different complexions of, 23–28; in US Census, 91
Rainbow, as emblem of South Africa, 97–98; as symbol of diversity, 100–101
Rawls, John, 81, 82
Rousseau, Jean-Jacques, 81
Rudolf II, Holy Roman Emperor, 35

Sexual selection, 74–76
Smith, Adam, 55, 113
Sowerby, George Brettingham, 69
Suleiman the Magnificent, 28

Tree of life, Darwin on, 49–50, 66–67; 65
Tutu, Desmond, 97

US Supreme Court, 92–97

Values, different realms of (see also Beauty, Efficiency, Justice), 1–5, 11–13; wandering, 2–3, 12, 109–111, 114; cumulative weight of, 86, 101–102, 110–111
Voltaire (François-Marie Arouet), 37

Weiditz, Christopher, 28, 30, 31, 39, 40
Wollstonecraft, Mary, 81
Wonder, 77–80
Worm, Olaus, 34
Wunderkammer, 33–38, 77